WHAT TO SAY TO GOD

365 DAYS OF INTIMACY WITH THE LORD

Wendy Harbour

WestBow Press books may be ordered through booksellers or by contacting:

WestBow Press
A Division of Thomas Nelson & Zondervan
1663 Liberty Drive
Bloomington, IN 47403
www.westbowpress.com
1 (866) 928-1240

ISBN: 978-1-5127-7533-4 (sc)
ISBN: 978-1-5127-7534-1 (hc)
ISBN: 978-1-5127-7532-7 (e)

Library of Congress Control Number: 2017902170

Print information available on the last page.

WestBow Press rev. date: 9/26/2017

I dedicate this book to my family.
Thank you for your love
and constant support.
It is through the words we say to God
and the power of the Holy Spirit
that the Lord brings about
change in our lives.
Keep on praying…

Inspired by:

Katy York and Kathleen Barley

Foreword

by Shelia Brown

What a delight to read a devotional that will bring the reader into an intimate dialog with the Lover of their soul! And what a blessing it is for me that this author, Wendy, is able to put in words how she has come to know how her God and Savior feels about her, and He is enough! May all who read this devotional be as blessed.

Introduction

Have you ever wanted to talk to God, but you just could not find the right words to say? I had been doing that very thing myself just about my whole life until a few years ago. I would never know what to say to God in prayer. I would say some very general prayers. I would say some repetitive prayers. I would even say prayers that I heard someone else saying. Then God revealed to me that talking to Him is not as difficult as I was making it out to be. Talking to Him should not be intimidating. It does not have to be repetitive, or general. It especially should not be a dreaded task or even someone else's thoughts. Although we make it out to be these things sometimes, talking to God can actually be quite simple, enlightening and refreshing. We should be eager to converse with our Maker each day. So what does that look like?

As a parent, I am overjoyed when my children come to me and want to talk about things. Imagine with me for a moment a young child stopping in the middle of whatever they are doing and coming to their parent. They begin to tell them how wonderful of a parent they have been. They say how magnificent and awesome all the things are that they have taught them. Then they start quoting things the parents have said to them and promises they have made through the years. The child then begins to honor and thank them for these abundant blessings. What if the child even went so far as to bow down in front of the parent and worship them? If you are a parent, can you even dream of the feeling that might stir in your heart? What if the child did this everyday in a fresh new way? That would be an amazing blessing to a parent! Think of how much more our Father in heaven will be blessed by our adoration and praise to Him for the things He has done in our lives. Think of how much more we, as His children, will be blessed by Him as we take moments out of our busy schedules to praise Him, reflect on what He has done, and show Him gratitude for what He has done and what He is going to do.

We know that an earthly child/parent relationship is unlikely to look exactly like the type of relationship we have with God the Father. It can be difficult for us to find new ways to praise God each morning because, let's face it, life can be a busy, redundant routine sometimes. So, how do we nurture our relationship with God in the busyness of life? How do we keep from being routine in our relationship with Him? We do it with praise, scripture and prayer. That is exactly what this book is designed to help us do, so that we can have a meaningful, intimate encounter with God every day of the year.

Our heavenly Father loves to be praised. He longs for His children to glorify His name. He waits for us to come and spend time with Him, sit at His feet and give Him glory for who He is and what He has done for us. He is patient for us to lift His name up in praise and adoration as we begin each day. He desires that we give Him thanks and appreciation for the many blessings He has chosen to share with us. He wants us to give Him glory for waking us up in the morning. He longs to hear from His children as well as speak to us.

Gratitude should be the main focus of our conversations with God. Oftentimes when we pray, it is easy to get caught up in asking God for things. We may say things like, "Lord, can You just give me this?" or "Lord, can You just fix that?" Many times our prayers are more focused on what our current needs are rather than on gratitude. Our focus should be turned more toward thanking and praising Him for the things He has already done. It will be more comfortable for us to continue in our relationship with Him by lining up with what His will is for our present situations and having a heart of gratitude along the way. He already knows everything about us. He knows every detail. He knows what we are dealing with and what the outcome will be. We can have peace through all circumstances by trusting Him and giving Him honor daily. Being thankful moves our focus off of ourselves and what our needs are, and puts the focus on God, where it should be.

Jesus knelt down and prayed in the garden before He was arrested, "Father if You are willing, take this cup from me; yet not My will but Yours be done" (Luke 22:42). After this prayer the Bible says an angel from heaven appeared to Him and strengthened Him. It is in those times when we feel like we are in anguish that this perfect model prayer that Jesus lifted up to His Father should be on *our* lips. I want angels to come from heaven and strengthen me when I pray this prayer. I trust we all do. The Lord knew we, like Jesus, would undergo extreme persecution from a world of darkness. Where else but on our knees in prayer to our Creator will we be able to draw strength in our time of weakness? I believe that Jesus would not have had the adequate amount of strength to make it through His suffering had He not prayed to God in heaven for strength in His hour of despair. The relationship of a child being dependent upon their parent is made complete through this illustration. It is imperative that we follow His perfect example to us.

When we choose to fully believe in God and believe His Word in its entirety, we step directly into righteousness. That is a great thought. We are righteous in the sight of the Lord! However, we may not always *feel* righteous. Sometimes the idea of being righteous takes longer for some of us to grasp than others. We all come from different backgrounds, and we all have different stories, but we are all called to walk with Jesus in righteousness when we choose to make Him Lord of our lives. By studying His Word, praying, and listening for His voice, we are taking steps toward a meaningful relationship with our Father that is like nothing else we will ever experience here on this earth. When we begin to know Jesus, righteousness will start to flow naturally and freely from our own heart's desire.

We are designed to love God and to be loved by God. He created us for His glory and His purposes. It is our responsibility to walk in the truth He has presented to us through the Bible. He has provided the Holy Spirit to speak to us individually and to be our helper and comforter.

When we choose to accept Christ as our Savior, it opens our minds to the wisdom of the Father. We then are able to receive knowledge, wisdom, and understanding that can only come from God Almighty Himself, who gives generously to His children. If you have never asked Jesus to be the Lord of your life, I would strongly suggest you pray to Him and do so before you begin reading the daily conversations contained in this book. However, if you choose to read this book before becoming a Christian you will most likely become a believer very soon after you begin reading. ☺

Most of the writings in this book are taken straight from God's Word. They are meant to bless the Lord and bless you as you read. There is no specific format that we are required to talk to God in, as long as it is from our heart. Sometimes we may feel as though we just cannot find the right words to say. This book helps put into words some of the things that are in the depths of our heart, yet we struggle to express. These thoughts are inspired by the Holy Spirit. I invite you to read slowly and meditate on each sentence. Discern where each reading fits into your own life circumstances, and allow the Holy Spirit to open your mind to what He wants *you* to say to Him. Let Him show you what He wants you to pray about. Please add your own words and personalize each prayer. God already knows what you are dealing with so speak from your heart. Praise Him, plead with Him, and thank Him for all things. We can only know what to say to God by reading His Word and opening our heart to the Spirit.

It is no secret that we are living in spiritual warfare. This 365 day devotional offers a daily guideline on how to praise God, how to be thankful for ways He has blessed you, and how to express sincere spiritual truths to Him. It also outlines many truths about ourselves. It teaches us who we are in Christ. It reveals what the Bible says about who God says we are. We are overwhelmed in this day and age with hurtful insults and crude comments. We must rebuke the enemy and speak life into our souls. Truth and life are found in the word of God. God's Living Word is the sword of the Spirit that will enable us to stand firm. Prayer is the key to fighting any battle. We can be confident that we are not fighting alone. God is on our side, and He will never leave us, and He will never forsake us (Hebrews 13:5). God created each individual to fulfill a purpose here on His earth. It is crucial that we not walk in defeat when He has already defeated the enemy. We are to walk in the victory that has already been won by our Savior. It will be much easier to deal with spiritual warfare if we will make a conscious choice to believe that our victory has already been won by our Lord and Savior, Jesus Christ.

A good time to read this devotional is sometime in the morning, although any time of day will encourage and inspire you. However, the way we start each day has much to do with how we look at our circumstances throughout the day. Choices we make during any given day are inspired by what we have already experienced that morning. Also, when we start our day by being uplifted, we are more likely to make sound decisions and to be an encouragement to those around us.

Speaking words of love and encouragement over yourself, especially when taken from the inspired word of God, has many advantages. It starts your day out right, puts positive thinking in your mind, and helps you feel important and close to the Lord Jesus Christ. These benefits will be a blessing to you, and they will increase as you read daily. This will also cause you to be a blessing to those around you. You will begin to notice that your blessings will start to overflow into others. What better way to spend your day. Positive thinking often seems difficult to achieve in the world we live in unless we are constantly exposed to it. With so many negative comments and attitudes in our society today, it is critical that we take time to be encouraged and experience positive thinking before we are bombarded with whatever the day may bring. Our outlook will be built up confidently when we are exposing ourselves to optimistic spiritual readings and prayers. We can attain spiritual growth and development through meaningful time spent with God in prayer and in scripture.

Obviously the Bible is the best tool ever written to provide fulfillment for all our needs and guidelines on how to live. That should always be our first book of reference. I encourage you to pray each morning, read the Bible, read the daily conversation to God, spend time saying what the Lord lays upon your heart, and listen with your full attention set on God. Try starting off with sitting quietly for at least one minute after you have read and prayed. Then I invite you to increase your time being still in His presence and focusing your mind on Him alone, so that you may go deeper into your relationship with the King of Kings. I also encourage you to bring a journal to record any profound thoughts or words the Lord may speak to you while you are listening and resting in Him. This is a great way to remember truths God has taught you, and you can always refer back to what you have written for confirmation of His promises to you personally. Also, if you have a smart phone please consider downloading a Bible app to make reading the scripture references at the top of each page easier and more efficient. This book was written to be read alongside God's Holy Word.

Having intimacy with God is a vital part of our relationship with Him. Look at it this way. When two people meet, (a potential husband and wife) they begin to get to know one another by being around each other. They spend time together. They express their thoughts, desires, dreams, ambitions and visions with one another. Over time they begin to fall in love and eventually become engaged. Romance, love, laughter, and long conversations become the norm. Then the time comes when they become united to one another in Holy Matrimony. This is when the real fun begins. This relationship between a husband and wife is very closely related to our relationship with Jesus. We hear about Jesus, we meet Him, we start spending time with Him, we express our deepest desires to Him, we fall in love with Him, we are engaged with Him, and the ultimate goal is to be united with Him. This relationship, however, is like no other. We must love God with all our heart, soul, mind, and strength before we can love others the way He intends for us to.

As you read the daily prayer, allow the Holy Spirit to interject thoughts about your own life and your personal circumstances. These readings are merely suggestions of what to say to God to bring you into conversation with Him each day. As we move into a closer walk with the Lord, we will go deeper into communication and relationship with Him. It is His desire that we praise Him. We should want to praise Him for what He has done for us. If we do not praise Him, the rocks will cry out to Him. That is just how Holy and magnificent He truly is.

I encourage you to start each day with praising the One who created the day. It is more than fulfilling to be able to praise God for the things He has done. It is life-changing to develop a heart of gratitude for God. In praising the Master daily you will see that everything else in your life will seem trivial and insignificant. Our God awaits our praises each morning as we rise to meet the day, and He inhabits the praises of His people. Let us give the Father the praise He is due in all that we are. Please be assured that I am praying for you each day as you discover what to say to God.

Read:
Romans 8:38–39

Intimacy

You and I Are One, God

I am enveloped with unspeakable joy today for You have captured my heart. You know the details of today and how everything will work out. I place my day in Your hands because I trust You, and I love You with all my heart. None other can captivate my mind and soul the way You do with Your everlasting love and remarkable Word. I praise You, my Father, for Your pursuance of my heart. Thank You for protecting it from the enemy and uniting it with Yours. Nothing can separate us. Neither death nor life, neither angels nor demons, neither height nor depth, nor anything else in all creation will be able to separate me from Your love, God, that is in Christ Jesus my Lord.

Thank You for this promise of truth . . .

Read:
Psalm 139:13–14; Ephesians 2:10

Worship

I Worship You, My King, Today

How beautiful are the works of Your hands. You are the master of artistic ability. The intricate details You put into images of Your world that my eyes are able to behold are breath-taking. You have created all things for Your glory, including me! I praise You for knitting me together in my mother's womb. I know full well that I was woven together by Your hands. Thank You for creating my inmost being. I am Your workmanship, created in Christ Jesus to do good works, which You prepared in advance for me to do. Thank You for planning my life from beginning to end, dear heavenly Father.

Thank You for choosing me to be a part of Your wondrous works of art . . .

Read:
**Psalm 91:1–2, 94:18–19; Luke 12:7;
Philippians 4:6–7**

Rest

I Am Dwelling in the Shelter of the Most High; Therefore, I Am Resting in the Shadow of the Almighty

You, God, are my refuge and fortress. I trust You. You guard my heart and my mind. You are Christ Jesus. You know my thoughts. You know how many hairs are on my head in each moment throughout the day. You know the depths of my heart, and You continue to love me. Your love supports me when my foot slips each day. You bring consolation and joy to my soul when anxiety is great within me. Who else could protect me from danger and trouble? You, O God, are my safe place. I find relief in You. I can escape the ways of the world by finding peace and comfort in Your presence. Thank You, Jesus, that I am of great worth in Your eyes.

I am resting in You . . .

Read:
Ephesians 4:21–24, 5:1–2

Available

I Am Thankful That You Make Yourself Available to Me, Christ Jesus

When I heard about You and Your truths, I knew I wanted You to be Lord of my life. My former way of life is gone. I have put off my old self. I have been made new in the attitude of my mind. I have put on the new self, created to be like You, God, in true righteousness and holiness. Now I am an imitator of God. I am a dearly loved child. I am living a life of love, just as You love me and gave Yourself up for me as a fragrant offering and sacrifice to Your Father. You have taught me how to make myself available to You and to others. You are continuing to teach me Your truths every day as I sit in Your presence and read Your Word.

Thank You for being ever available to me . . .

Read:
Romans 1:17, 3:21–26

Righteous

You Are the Incredibly Holy God

Lord, Your Word tells me I am righteous. I *am* righteous. I live by faith. I believe in You, Jesus. I know I am a sinner, and I fall short of Your glory. I am justified freely by Your grace through the redemption that came by You, Jesus. You are the sacrifice of atonement. You shed Your blood so that I could be justified (just as if I had never sinned). I have faith that Your blood that was shed has forgiven my sins. My righteousness comes from You because my faith lies completely in You. You see me as holy and forgiven. I praise You for making me righteous. I give You honor for allowing me the opportunity to live by faith in You, Christ Jesus. You are worthy to be praised. You are holy in all Your ways. Thank You for making a way for me to live through You.

Thank You for making me righteous . . .

Read:
Proverbs 2:10; 1 Corinthians 1:4–9

Fellowship

God, I Am So Thankful for You

I am more grateful than ever for the grace that has been given me through Jesus Christ. I have been enriched in every way through the Holy Spirit living in me. The Spirit gives me knowledge in the way I speak and think. Lord, Your wisdom enters my heart, and knowledge is pleasant to my soul. Through my personal testimony, Your existence and truth is confirmed. I do not lack any spiritual gift as I eagerly wait for my Lord Jesus Christ to be revealed. You will keep me strong to the end, so that I will be blameless on the day of my Lord Jesus Christ. You have called me into fellowship with Your son Jesus Christ my Lord. And You, God, are faithful.

Your faithfulness to me brings pleasure to my soul . . .

Read:
Psalm 1; Hebrews 13:5

Your Presence

I Invite Your Presence Into My Life, Heavenly Father

You are high and lifted up in everything I do. I recognize that You are my Lord and Savior. You are my King of Kings and Lord of Lords. You are an astounding God. It is good to be alive during this global movement of Your Holy Spirit. Thank You for calling me blessed. My delight is in Your law. I meditate on it day and night. I am like a tree planted by streams of water, which yields its fruit in season, and my leaves do not wither. Whatever I do prospers, and I am content with what I have. You are watching over the way of the righteous. You are faithful to Your people. You will never leave me. You will never forsake me. Thank You for loving me.

Thank You for Your constant holy presence in my life, Jesus . . .

Read:
Matthew 24:13; Romans 9:17; Ephesians 2:10

Belonging

I Show Honor to You This Day, Father

You have done good things to me. I am fully Yours, Lord. By the grace of God, I am what I am. I have been made alive in You, Christ. Everything is placed under You. I am part of Your glorious creation. When You look at me, You see Your splendor. I will stand firm to the end, and You will let nothing move me. I have given myself fully to the work of Your hands, Lord. Nothing I do is in vain because You have created me to be raised up in power and glory. I will proclaim Your name in all the earth. Thank You for giving me a purpose in this life.

Thank You, Lord, for showing me that I belong to You . . .

Read:
Exodus 3:5; Proverbs 3:6

Your Will

Today is Your Creation, O Mighty God of Heaven and Earth

Do with this day what You will. Do with *me* what You will. I am fully and completely Yours. I am standing in Your presence on holy ground. I acknowledge You in all my ways. Refresh the areas of my life that have become stagnant and dull. Forgive my sluggish ways, and give me strength to face the challenges set before me today. I do not wish to be inactive in Your kingdom work, but I long for a lead role in the development and advancement of Your people. I want to see a progressive movement of the Spirit in Your world today. Keep me aligned with Your purposes so that we can accomplish these things together, while we enjoy sweet fellowship with one another along the way.

I am so thankful and glad to be walking in Your will, Father . . .

Read:
Psalm 40:1–3

Love

I Am Amazed at the Ways You Love Me

Lord, You are worthy of all things. You are amazing me every day. All I am to do is wait patiently on You, and You will turn to me. You will hear me when I cry every time without fail. You have lifted my life out of the slimy pit, out of the mud and mire. You have set my feet on a rock and given me a firm place to stand. What is even better than that, is that You have put a new song in my mouth, a hymn of praise just for Yourself. You care so much about me that You would rescue me from whatever trouble I am having in this world, and then put music and joy in me. It comes out of my mouth, into Your ears, and it makes You happy.

You really love me, God. Thank You . . .

Read:
Philippians 4:7

Peace

You Are the Prince of Peace, Father God

You are so close to me, Lord. I feel Your love surrounding me. I feel peace in my heart. You have placed it there with Your loving hands. I am peaceful, and I am able to endure a disrupted life because of the peace You have given me. I am aware that this is a fallen world I live in and that peace can be scarce. However, the peace You impart passes all understanding, and it guards my heart and my mind. You give peace in abundance to those of us who will ask for it, acknowledge it, and receive it. Thank You, Father, for placing a generous supply of peace in my heart. It helps me through each day. Truly You are my Savior, and You are so close to me.

Thank You for Your peace . . .

Read:
Psalm 40:3; Matthew 11:28; John 16:33;
Romans 5:20; 1 Corinthians 15:55;
2 Corinthians 12:9; Hebrews 12:2

Grace

God, Your Grace is Greater Than Any Sin

You are way bigger than any little thing that afflicts me. I am absolutely aware that difficulty and disorder are always ready to upset me. I acknowledge that pain and trouble are a part of any given human life here in this fallen world, yet my discomfort does not have a hold on me. My anguish and sufferings are in Your hands. They belong to You because You have invited me to lay my burdens at Your feet. I will not be tormented throughout my days because You have taken on my distress. You have endured my pain, and You did it with joy in Your heart. You did it with love for me. You have inspired me to walk proudly with a new song in my mouth. I will live victoriously throughout my days knowing that You are alive. Death has been defeated, and I will be with You in heaven one day. Thank You for hope, grace and forgiveness of sin. Thank You for being my God and Savior.

Your grace is sufficient . . .

Read:
Isaiah 41:10; Joel 3:10; Ephesians 2:10

Strength

You Are Strength, Lord

All my strength comes from You, God. I am weak. I admit that I am not strong in any way without You. I can only say I am strong because of Your strength You have graciously and willingly shared with me. You have planted an inner strength deep down in the depths of my being, so that I can make it through this life. It is only by that strength that I can accomplish the works You line up for me to do each day. When I begin to praise You, as I awake in the morning, Your strength immediately begins to fill up this weak, tired and weary vessel. The more I praise, the more strength You pour out on me. I can stand because You are holding me up with Your righteous right hand. It is Your hand that gives me strength and helps me. Thank You, God, for giving me strength and help.

Thank You, Lord, for upholding and strengthening me . . .

Read:
Psalm 115:15; John 14:2–4; 2 Corinthians 5:1–5

Heaven

Lord, You Are the Maker of Heaven and Earth

You have prepared a home for me in heavenly places. I long to gaze into these things that are to come. My earthly tent You have provided is but temporary. I have great confidence that I have an eternal house in heaven, not built by human hands. I have a yearning to be clothed with my heavenly dwelling. I realize I have been called by You for many influential purposes. You have made me to accomplish great things, and Your Spirit living in me, is a deposit of what is to come. You have guaranteed me a place in Your Kingdom. I am richly engaged with Your intentions for my life. You are keeping me focused on Your plan as I start each day. The wonder of what is to come is my motivation to please You in all I do. Thank You for this extraordinary privilege.

Thank You for the preparations You are making in heaven this very hour . . .

Read:
Psalm 147:1–6, 14

Creation

I Praise You, My God, Who Makes the Wind Blow and the Waters Flow

It is pleasant and fitting for me to give You my highest praises. You send out Your command to the earth, and Your Word runs swiftly. Your Word strengthens me. You have blessed my territory and made peace in my borders. I am delighted to be Your child. You have healed my broken heart and bound up my wounds. You have lifted up the humble, and You cast down the wicked. You count the number of the stars, and You call them all by name. Great are You Lord, and mighty in power. Your understanding is infinite. Thank You for creating wonder in my heart so that I may praise You all day long. Your world is so beautiful!

Thank You for allowing me to live here and settle in Your presence . . .

Read:
Psalm 124

Worship

Blessed Be Your Name

Lord, You have made a way for me. As I lift praises to You, God, Your Holy Spirit ushers me closer into Your presence to a place of sincere intimacy with You. This is where I love to be. My heart responds to You with worship. You are on my side, Lord. My soul has escaped many snares because my help is in the name of the Lord. I exalt You for what You have done. My response to Your goodness is made complete in worship. I know Your heart loves me. I feel loved by You, Father. I express my deepest love and adoration for You when I am prostrate at Your feet. My mouth cannot even utter words. Your manifest presence brings me to a place of reverence and peace.

Thank You for this special time of worship we share . . .

Read:
Psalm 39:12; Psalm 90:10; James 4:13–15

Friend

You Are With Me, God

You never leave me while I am on this path through life. I am traveling with my True Friend. You are a faithful companion. I am never alone. You are always in my midst. I am a stranger in this world. I dwell with You, yet I am as an alien, a foreigner in this world. Though there may be trouble and sorrow, You hear my prayer, O Lord. You listen to my cry for help. You are not deaf to my weeping. My time here passes quickly. I am living under Your will for my life. What will happen today and tomorrow is in Your hands, Jesus. I am a mist that appears for a little while and then vanishes, yet I have great confidence in You, God, my Lord and Savior. Thank You for always walking with me through each day. Thank You for being my partner through this uncertain life.

Thank You for being my friend . . .

Read:
Lamentations 3:22, 32–33

Love

You Have Wrapped Me Up in Your Love, Jesus

My love for You is increasing because of this wonderful act of kindness I have received from You. Even though this world can be a sorrowful place, I know where to run to receive healing and grace. I know I will face many hardships. It is through these trials that I learn to lean into my Savior. This is where I find Your unfailing love. You do not willingly bring affliction, however, You have shown me great compassion, and great is Your love for me, Father.

Thank You for teaching me how to love You through the way You love me . . .

Read:
Deuteronomy 31:8

Your Presence

I Praise You for Your Presence, Father

You are always with me, Lord. No matter what I am going through, You are here to see me through it, Lord. You walk with me in dark and lonely places, as well as in bright and joyful ones. Your presence is with me even when I am unhappy, angry, bitter or resentful. It is in these times when I feel Your presence coming through the strongest in me. What could ever bring me back to joy and peace other than You, a loving God? You teach me how to deal with my feelings. Your gentle and caring Spirit speaks to me softly as I ask for forgiveness and direction. Thank You, Father, for restoring me and holding me up high. Thank You for seeing me through all of life's ups and downs.

Thank You for never giving up on me . . .

Read:
1 John 3:1, 4:1–16

Love

You Are a God That Never Stops Loving Me

I praise You for the gift of love. I rely on Your love, Lord. How great is the love You have lavished on me, that I should be called a child of God. I have been born of You, and I love You. *You* are love, Lord. I know what love is because You showed me. Through sending Jesus, I know just how loved I really am. You did this so that I could live through Him. Jesus is the atoning sacrifice for my sin. Since You love me so much, I must choose to love others. By doing this Your love is made complete in me. Help me to love others, for love comes from You, God. Thank You for Your Spirit that lives in me. Thank You for always loving me.

Thank You for helping me acknowledge that Jesus Christ has come in the flesh as God, and He is the One who taught the world to love . . .

Read:
Psalm 16:11; Psalm 81:10; Colossians 2:6–10

Filled

You Are the One True God That Fills Me to Overflowing

You are the Source that fills me with joy. I have been given fullness in You, Christ. I overflow with thankfulness. I have received You as Lord. I am rooted and built up in You. You are my strength. You fill me with joy in Your presence, with eternal pleasures at Your right hand. All of Your fullness lives inside of me, Jesus. You are the head of every power and authority. My mouth is open wide that You may fill it. I am depending on You each day for this fulfilling satisfaction. I delight in coming to the fountain to get my supply. I am overwhelmed by Your ability to fill me up in fresh new ways each time I am thirsty and hungry. Thank You for supplying what is lacking in me.

Thank You for inundating me with Your joy . . .

Read:
Deuteronomy 33:26; Philippians 4:4;
1 Thessalonians 5:18

Thankfulness

There is No One Like You, God

You ride on the heavens to help me and on the clouds in Your majesty. I am blessed with Your good gifts from Your powerful mighty hand. I praise You, Lord! My blessings far outweigh my adversity. It is not difficult for me to look into my life and begin to count each blessing and gift from You, Father. I will take time out of my busy schedule to do it. As I focus my mind on gratitude, my heart will rejoice in the Lord. You have granted me more than I can say in words. Your desire is for me to have a grateful heart; I want a heart full of thanksgiving and gratitude. I have plenty, and I am blessed. Thank You for reaching into me and refocusing my heart toward the blessings You give.

Thank You, Jesus, for blessing me . . .

Read:
Job 1:21; Isaiah 61:1–3; James 1:12

Generosity

I Give Glory and Thanks to You, Father, for Another Day in Your World

You are the God who gives and takes away. Blessed is Your name. You give to me abundantly. You give love, mercy, grace, truth, forgiveness, wisdom and freedom. You take away hate, wrath, falsehood, iniquities, darkness and bondage. You bind up the brokenhearted, and give freedom for the captives. You give me a crown of beauty instead of ashes and a garment of praise instead of a spirit of despair. Thank You, Lord, for blessing me with the promise that I will receive the crown of life because I have loved You.

Thank You for Your everlasting generosity . . .

Read:
Ephesians 3:14–21

Your Presence

I Kneel Before You, My Father

Out of Your glorious riches, You strengthen me with power through Your Spirit in my inner being. Through my faith, You are able to dwell in my heart. I am rooted and established in love. I have power, together with all the saints, to grasp how wide and how long and how high and how deep Your love is for me. I am engulfed in this love that surpasses knowledge, and I am filled to the measure of all the fullness of You, God. You are able to do immeasurably more than all I ask or imagine, according to Your power that is at work within me. All glory is given to You, Christ Jesus, throughout all generations for ever and ever!

Thank You for Your glorious presence . . .

Read:
Romans 5:1–8

Grace

There is No Other Grace Giver Like You, Holy God

I have gained access into grace by having faith in You, Jesus. I have peace with You. I am thankful that I have been justified through faith. I rejoice in the hope of the glory of You, my Lord. I also rejoice in my sufferings because I know that suffering produces perseverance. Perseverance produces character, and character produces hope. Hope does not disappoint me because You have poured out Your love into my heart by the Holy Spirit You have given me. You have demonstrated Your love for me by dying for me even though You already knew I was going to be a sinner. What amazing love You have for me! What unspeakable joy I have because I believe this truth.

Thank You, Jesus, for helping me understand Your grace for me . . .

Read:
1 Corinthians 2:10–16; James 1:5

Wisdom

You Are Wise, Sovereign Father

All wisdom comes from You. You are the only One from whom I receive divine wisdom. You reveal Your wisdom to me when I ask for it. You give Your wisdom to me generously. I am able to understand Your wisdom because You have given me Your Spirit who teaches me. Your Spirit has expressed spiritual truths to me in spiritual words. I accept the things that come to me from Your Spirit. I can understand them, as You have given me spiritual discernment. You have given me the mind of Christ.

Thank You, heavenly Father, for granting me spiritual wisdom, knowledge and truth . . .

Read:
Exodus 9:16; Matthew 8:26; Acts 4:30–31;
Matthew 17:20; Colossians 3:17; Titus 2:15

Your Name

I Will Proclaim Your Name in All the Earth

There is power in Your name, Jesus! All authority comes from You. When I say Your name I can move mountains. Your name has the power to calm the raging seas. Your name is above all names. No other name has power over anything in heaven or on earth like the name of Jesus. You have given me Your name to use. You have granted me authority and permission to use Your name when I need it. You are my Father, and I am Your child. Whatever is in Your Kingdom belongs to me. I can use the power and authority of Your name in my circumstances. No matter what I am facing Your name is stronger and more powerful. I can defeat anything because You have shared with me the power that resides in You. That same power is in me because You are in me. Thank You, Jesus!

I am thankful Your name is so mighty . . .

Read:
John 6:35; John 7:37–38; Galatians 5:22–25

Filled

Lord, You Are the Bread of Life and the Living Water That Fills My Soul

I come to You, Lord, and I never go hungry. I believe in You, and I am never thirsty, Jesus. Let rivers of living water flow from within me today. I will not be consumed with what this world has to offer me to eat or drink. You, Holy God, are my source of strength. May I only crave the goodness You offer. May my stomach only long to be filled with Your fruit that comes from the Spirit. I belong to You, Jesus. I am living by the Spirit. I am keeping in step with the Spirit. Thank You for feeding me good things.

Thank You for quenching my dry mouth and nourishing my hungry soul . . .

Read:
Proverbs 22:1; Daniel 12:1

My Name

You Know My Name, God

You have called me by my name. My name is found written in the book of life because You have placed it there. I am delivered by Your hand. My name is important to You. My name is good. It is more desirable than great riches. I am esteemed by You, and it is better than silver or gold. You find favor in me, and You have placed value in me. You hold me in high regard. I am Your child placed in this world by Your deep desire so that You may love me, and I may love You. Amen.

Thank You for calling me by name . . .

Read:
Isaiah 9:7; Zechariah 9:10; Colossians 3:15

Peace

There is No End to Your Peace, Mighty God

You reign with justice and righteousness. You proclaim peace to the nations, and Your rule extends from sea to sea and from the River to the ends of the earth. I am letting Your peace rule in my heart, and I am thankful. I am called to peace by You, Christ. You alone, Lord, are peaceful, and You distribute peace to me at all times and in every way. All I must do is take hold of the peace You bring to me. You are always right here waiting to incorporate order into my ways. May I acknowledge the peace You have freely granted to me each day. It is bountiful. It is unending. You are unending. I praise You, God of peace.

Thank You, Lord, for peace . . .

Read:
Psalm 147:18; Philippians 4:13;
Hebrews 12:2

Control

My Dear Heavenly Father, You Are in Control of This Day

Lord, You are able to take care of all the challenges I am going to face on any given day. You already know what is going to happen and how things will turn out. You know everything! It is amazing that I serve an all-powerful, all-knowing God! My mind cannot contain the thought of it! Your majesty alone is what I worship. I stand in awe of You. I am so thankful that I do not have to try to make it through this day by myself. With my eyes continually fixed on You and what You are going to do, this day and all its challenges will be a breeze for me. That is just what You are, Father – a gentle breeze, so faithful to blow through at just the right time. Your Word melts my heart, and the waters begin to flow as I depend on You. I can do anything and everything because I draw the strength I need from You.

Thank You for being in control of this day . . .

Read:
Job 19:25; 2 Samuel 22:2; Isaiah 42:11

In Your Name

You Are Lord of My Whole Life

You are Lord of all! I submit everything I am to You, God. You carry me through all things. I know there is power in Your Name. I have declared many things in my life, in the Name of Jesus. I am given this freedom by You, Father. Many chains have been broken and will continue to break and fall, in the Name of Jesus, in my life and in the lives around me. I will not be ashamed of what You have done for me. I will proclaim Your goodness from the mountaintops. Who can stop me! You are my deliverer and my redeemer! I am proud to call You my Lord and Savior. Thank You, Jesus. Thank You for this privilege.

You are an amazing Father . . .

Read:
Psalm 22:10–11; Psalm 139:7–10;
Matthew 28:20; Hebrews 10:23

Your Presence

Lord, You Are Everywhere, All the Time

You are never far from me. I have security in You. God, I know that You are with me always. You have been with me even before I was born. Even though my mind often wanders, You are there in the wandering places. In the time when I lose my focus, Your gentle Spirit always ushers me back to where You want me to be. Your right hand holds me fast. You are kind in dealing with me each day. Your love makes it possible for me to trust in Your promises. You are faithful to Your promises. Thank You for making it attainable for me to be with You always. Thank You for all Your kindness toward me, even when my attention is on other things. Thank You for delicately redirecting me back to Your love and goodness.

Thank You for being present with me
throughout each of my days . . .

Read:
Psalm 91:11; Philippians 4:6–7

Prayer

Thank You for Prayer, God

I thank You, Jesus, for answering me. Your Holy Spirit is my great comforter. You take away my hurt. You send Your healing angels. They guard me in all my ways. You accomplish great things through my prayers. When I call upon Your name, I feel the love You have for me. All I have to do is open my mouth and say the name of Jesus, and Your power begins to work through me. The things that can be achieved through the very mention of Your name are endless. Thank You for making Yourself available to me at all times through prayer. Thank You for peace and assurance. Thank You for Your comfort.

Thank You for prayer . . .

Read:
James 1:19–25

Righteousness

Father, You Are Pure

I worship You each day with thanksgiving, and I come to You with repentance in my heart. You desire my life to be righteous. You want me to be quick to listen, slow to speak and slow to become angry. Anger does not bring about the righteous life that You desire, God. Forgive me. I humbly accept the Word planted in me, which can save me from my sin. I will not only read and listen to Your Word, but I will do what it says. I will look intently into the perfect law that gives freedom. I will not forget what the Bible says. You will bless me in what I do. You accept me into Your loving arms.

Thank You for Your purity that brings me righteousness . . .

Read:
Joel 2:12–13

Grace and Compassion

You Are Gracious and Compassionate, God

You have to be so that You can deal with people like me. You want all of my heart, Lord. You want all of me. I want to yield my heart to You. The one thing I want to be broken for is You, Lord Jesus. Instead of returning to You after going about my own way, I want to be in complete submission to You whether I am at Your feet or going to and fro. You release this feeling of peace over me when I am in Your presence. It goes with me throughout my day. This is the only way I can deal with the things in front of me each day. Your presence changes everything. Thank You for lavishing Your love on me as I bow before Your grace and compassion. You wait quietly for me so that You can bless me.

Thank You for Your grace and compassion
on this imperfect frame . . .

Read:
2 Kings 17:38–39; Luke 19:40

Worship

Glory and Honor Belong to You, God

Your name will be high and lifted up. Your name will be praised. If Your people do not praise You, the stones will cry out praises unto You. That is just how majestic You are. I will only worship You, Lord. You will deliver me, and I will never forget what You have done. Keep me from the ways of this world so that I can give You my true, genuine heart of worship. May I never miss one moment of opportunity to give You the honor You are due. You are the great Lord of all creation. Thank You for choosing to create me so that I can praise You. All worship and adoration belong to the mighty name of Jesus!

Praise You, Father . . .

Read:
Psalm 13:5–6; Proverbs 19:22

Unfailing Love

I Sing to You, Lord

You have been good to me. I trust in Your unfailing love, Lord. My heart rejoices in Your salvation. My desire is to experience unfailing love which can only come from You, Father of all nations. Nothing in this world can satisfy my desires. There is but temporary fulfillment in man and in material possessions. But with You, Lord, I have eternal contentment. I rest in Your unfailing love, Lord. My peace is found in You, Jesus. Your love and faithfulness keep me safe. My trust is in Your unfailing love, Father. Thank You for securing me.

Thank You for Your unfailing love . . .

Read:
Psalm 84

Dwelling

Better is One Day in Your Courts Than a Thousand Elsewhere

Your dwelling place is lovely, Lord Almighty. My soul yearns, even faints, for Your courts, Father. My heart and my flesh cry out for You. You are the living God. I have set my heart on pilgrimage. My hope and strength are found in You. You carry me from strength to strength. You are a sun and shield for me. You bestow favor and honor. You do not withhold one good thing from those whose walk is blameless. How I trust in You, Lord. I am blessed in Your presence, and I will be found ever praising You, Lord of all.

Thank You for letting me dwell with You in the secret garden of life . . .

Read:
Genesis 1:1; Isaiah 40:28; 1 Peter 3:22

Submission

You Are the Beginning, God

You are the creator of the heavens and the earth. Angels, authorities and powers are in submission to You. I have heard, and I see and know that You are the everlasting God. You will not grow tired or weary. No one can fathom Your understanding. In knowing all this, I am desperately inclined to be in total submission to You, Lord. You hold all things in Your righteous hand. I am not here for me but for You and Your glory. I am Your creation, and I bow at Your throne. I submit to Your great authority and lordship over my life. Thank You for honoring my life with the presence of Your Holy Spirit that dwells inside of my soul. Thank You for thinking of me, Lord.

I am honored, and it brings me much pleasure to submit myself to You and to Your authority, Lord Jesus . . .

Read:
Romans 8:28, 36–37; Revelation 12:11

Overcoming

Lord, You Are the Ultimate Overcomer

Thank You, Jesus, for Your example to me by the way You overcame this world by death on a cross. What a great sacrifice You made for me personally. I know that I am an overcomer because You proved it can be accomplished. The word of my testimony regarding Your death and resurrection will go forth because I love You. I will continue to praise You in the storms of life, for Your Word tells me that I am more than a conqueror through Him who loves me. You know everything I face all day long, and in all these things You are working for my good because You love me. I am called according to Your purpose, not my own. I will overcome all things, for You have said I will. Thank You for this confidence I have. I look to You, Jesus.

Thank You for being my perfect example . . .

Read:
Romans 5:20

Grace

Christ, Your Grace is Greater Than All My Sin

You are faithful to give me relief from a heavy burden in my heart. I do not carry my sin around with me. I nail it to the cross where sins are forgiven. You have provided this method of forgiveness to Your child so that I may live freely and know what love is by Your Spirit that teaches me. Your affection toward me, by revealing this truth to me, has caused an emotion of passion to well up inside of me. I yearn to worship You, almighty Giver of life. Thank You for gracing me with Your presence among life's burdens

Thank You for grace . . .

Read:
1 Corinthians 4:1–5

Praise

Lord, I Praise You Today Because You Are Worthy To Be Praised

You deserve the most praise and honor of all. May Your name be lifted higher and higher each day. I am Your servant, Christ. You have entrusted me with the secret things. It is my responsibility to prove faithful with what You have given me. I am not disturbed with what man thinks of me. I should not even be concerned with what I think of myself. I am here for You alone. You are the reason for my existence. I know You are the ultimate Judge, and You will bring to light what is hidden in darkness. You will indeed expose the motives of my heart. May my life reflect that of Jesus Christ so that I may receive praise from You, Father. Until that day, I will praise You with all my heart and soul.

May everything that is in me give You praise . . .

Read:
Romans 5:1–8

Grace

There is No Other Grace Giver Like You, Holy God

I have gained access into grace by having faith in You. I have peace with You. I am thankful that I have been justified through faith. I rejoice in the hope of the glory of You. I also rejoice in my sufferings because I know that suffering produces perseverance. Perseverance produces character, and character produces hope. Hope does not disappoint me, because, God, You have poured out Your love into my heart by the Holy Spirit You have given me. You have demonstrated Your love for me by dying for me even though You already knew I was going to be a sinner. What amazing love You have for me! What unspeakable joy I have because I believe this truth.

Thank You, Jesus, for helping me understand Your grace for me . . .

Read:
1 Corinthians 13:4–8

Love

Jesus, Your Love Never Fails Me

Your love is patient and kind. It does not envy or boast, and it is never proud. Your love for me is not rude or self-seeking. You are not easily angered. You keep no record of my wrongs. Your love does not delight in evil, but rejoices with the truth. You always protect me. My hope is in You, and I am persevering daily. Thank You for the assurance that Your love will never fail me. Teach me to be patient and kind like You, Father. Forgive me when I envy, boast or act proud. Keep me from being rude, self-seeking, or angry. I declare today that I will not keep records of wrongdoings, and I will not delight in any evil, but I will rejoice with the truth always. Grant me the dignity and integrity to protect, trust, hope and persevere. I know this is the most excellent way.

Thank You for revealing Your love to me through Your Word . . .

Read:
Psalm 34:3; Matthew 6:9; Matthew 18:20;
John 16:24; Romans 10:13; Philippians 2:9;
Colossians 3:17

Your Name

Your Name is Above All Names, Lord

I will lift Your name high. I will exalt Your name together with Your people. I will praise the magnificent name of Jesus. Your name is Holy. I have called upon Your name, and You have saved me. Hallowed be Your name. We come together in Your name. We ask for everything in Your name. We ask and receive, and our joy is made complete in Your name. Our very existence is because of Your name. May everything I do be done in the name of my Lord Jesus. Thank You for giving me Your name.

Thank You for the power that is in me
because of Your great name . . .

Read:
Job 9:4; Romans 12:1

All I Am

God, You Are So Vast

I am so small. All I have to offer You is myself. I lay everything that I am at Your feet, precious Jesus. There is no thing in me that I can bring that even compares to Your greatness. You have created all that I am. I am weak, and You are mighty. The only reason I am here is because of You, God. Your strong hand has made all things the way they are. I honor You by laying my life before You. I adore You, Abba Father. Thank You for allowing me the privilege of bringing my all to You. I know You look upon me with love and acceptance, and You are pleased with me. Thank You, God. I love You.

Thank You for loving me just as I am . . .

Read:
Psalm 34:18; Psalm 35:10; Proverbs 3:5–6; Isaiah 61:1

Available

You Are Everywhere, Holy God

You are in the streets. You are with the poor. You are inside of me. Your presence is all over the whole earth. You have made Yourself available. May I acknowledge You in all my ways. You are among the broken, the sick, and the afflicted. You are there. You want to heal. You want to redeem. You want to show love. I am Your vessel. I can go to the streets, to the poor, to the broken, and to the sick and afflicted. You have called me to go and pray, and love Your children. You will be with me. You will heal. You will redeem. You will show them Your love, O holy One. In Your name all things will be done. In Your name great and powerful movements will be seen. May Your love be poured out through Your Holy Spirit that resides in me. May I be continually available to serve You and Your children in the name of Jesus.

Thank You for being available wherever I am . . .

Read:
Matthew 4:23–24; Matthew 12:15; 3 John 2

Healing

God, You Are the Giver of Health and Life

You heal every sickness and disease. Not only do You heal *my* little sicknesses, You heal *all* the sick in Your world. Every healing comes from You, Jesus. My soul is getting along well because of Your healings that have taken place in me. I cannot make it through one day without Your healing touch. You heal my mind. You heal my body. You are my strength. You are the Great Physician. May I never get over depending on You for healing in any area of my life. Jesus, You hold the healing touch that many long for. Give me boldness to tell of Your sanative ways. Thank You for Your healing touch that enthralls me each day.

Thank You for placing the desire inside of me to depend on You for all my healing . . .

Read:
Psalm 22:3; Ezekiel 37:5; 2 Corinthians 5:17

Your Presence

Lord, You Are Enthroned as The Holy One

Thank You Lord for inhabiting my praises. You are what keeps me going each day. You are the strength I need to overcome this life. I am so grateful for Your presence that surrounds me. Thank You for taking up residence in this empty body made from dust. It is only through Your Holy Spirit living inside of me that I am able to stand. It is only through You that I can lift my eyes and sing praises to Your name. Thank You, Jesus, for bringing my dry bones to life each morning. Thank You for raising me up to new strength in You each time I begin to praise Your holy name. I am a new creation.

Thank you for Your presence that gives me a new life through Jesus Christ . . .

Read:
Psalm 47

Creation

I Shout to You, God, With Cries of Joy

How awesome are You, Lord Most High! I bring my hands together for You, the great King over all the earth! I sing praises to You, God my King! The people of the earth belong to You, God. May they accept their position in Your family and receive their inheritance. I recognize that You are the Creator of life and everything else. Who but You, Father of all nations, could have done such mighty works? I stand in awe of You, Abba. Thank You for Your creations.

Thank You for allowing me to praise the works of Your hands . . .

Read:
Romans 3:21–22;
1 Corinthians 1:30; 1 John 1:9

Righteousness

God, You Are the Perfect Picture of What a True Father Looks Like

When You look at me, You see purity and innocence, the way an earthly parent should look at their own flesh and blood, remembering that their child was created by You and belongs to You. I praise You for holding me in a position of righteousness before You. You have made me complete in all my ways. I thank You for cleansing me of guilt and making me worthy to be in Your presence. Thank You for being a true, loving and just God and Father. Thank You for holding me and loving me like a father should.

You are a perfect, righteous God and Father . . .

Read:
Psalm 27:14; Isaiah 43:19; Acts 2:2

Worship

Praise to You, Lord

I am so thankful to You for this moment in time that I get to spend with You. I am confident that my day will be better now that I am taking this portion of it to worship You. In Your presence, I am stricken with such a powerful, yet peaceful force from You. I can feel the magnitude of Your supremacy enter into my spirit as I sit quietly and adore You. Your wind blows from heaven and fills my temple. You are able to do new and wonderful things with me during this time. You make a pathway in the wilderness, and You place streams in the dry wasteland. What an effective impact this has on me. I can sense things better and hear You speaking to me more clearly as I wait for You. This precious time we spend together is vital for me to be able to carry out the work You are trying to do here on earth.

I thank You for every available moment I have been given to spend worshipping You, Jesus . . .

Read:
Exodus 16:4; Ephesians 6:17;
2 Timothy 3:16–17

Equipped

Lord, I Bow Down Before You This Day

I worship who You are. You are the One my heart is in love with. You provide me with the manna that You rain down from heaven each morning, and I gather with great delight. You have equipped me with strength to go forward. You have awakened my soul to Your truths, and I am thanking You for it. You have equipped me for every good work through Your scriptures which are God-breathed. Your word is useful for teaching, rebuking, correcting, and training in righteousness. Thank You for the Sword of the Spirit. I am thankfully equipped through the One I love.

Thank You for providing and supplying . . .

Read:
Matthew 3:11; 1 Thessalonians 5:19;
Hebrews 12:29

Consuming Fire

You Are a Consuming Fire, Lord Jesus

You are what sets me ablaze. Our individuality is intensely combined through the flames of Your love. You placed powerful emotions inside of me when I became baptized with Your Holy Spirit and with fire. Where Your Spirit is there is fire. I chose to invite Your Spirit's fire to live inside of me when I asked You to become my Lord and Savior. No, I will not put out the Spirit's fire, but I will let it burn brightly, and I will pray that it spreads like a wildfire. You are living in me, and I am consumed by You. This kind of combustion is exactly what this darkened world needs. Thank You for giving me the privilege of spreading the fire. Thank You for setting me ablaze.

Thank You for consuming me . . .

Read:
1 Chronicles 16:34; Isaiah 40:22

Provision

I Give Thanks to You, Lord

You are good! Your love endures forever! You sit enthroned above the circle of the earth. You stretch out the heavens like a canopy over Your people. You provide everything fit to be eaten which nourishes every member of the human race that You created. We are Your people, and we entrust our lives to Your Holy Kingdom. We yearn to fellowship with You throughout our days. You are continually with us. Thank You for making preparations for our well-being. Thank You for extending Your love to Your people through the gospel of Jesus Christ. You have given us all we need in every way.

Thank You for Your deep compassion,
love, and sincere care . . .

Read:
Psalm 81:6, 16; Psalm 103:4; Isaiah 53:6

Redemption

I Shout Praises to You, Lord My God, for the Things You Have Done

You redeemed my life from the pit and set my feet upon a solid rock. Like a sheep gone astray, You lead me back to a safe place because You love me, and You care about me. You are my rescuer. You answer me when I call out to You. You feed me with the finest and satisfy me with the best. You have set me free and removed the burdens from my shoulders. I praise Your holy name. Thank You for Your wonder-working power that emerges in my daily activities because Your Spirit is living within me.

Thank You for redeeming me . . .

Read:
Jeremiah 31:3; Song of Songs 5:16

Love

You Are Everything to Me, Father

I was created to worship You. You love me beyond what my mind can conceive. I take pleasure in being in Your presence. Our relationship grows stronger and deeper every time we come together. It is the most perfect love story ever written. You are my all in all, and I am loved by You with an everlasting love. I find joy in giving myself to You each day. I am thankful that You draw me gently with unfailing kindness. I am Your beloved, and You are my flawless One. You are altogether lovely. I cherish everything You are to me.

Thank You, my Lord, for loving me . . .

Read:
1 Corinthians 2:16; Colossians 2:6–10

Salvation

I Have Received You, Christ Jesus, as Lord Over My Life

I continue to live in You, rooted and built up in You. I am strengthened in my faith, and I am overflowing with thankfulness. No one can take me captive with hollow and deceptive philosophy. I have the mind of Christ! I do not depend on human tradition or the basic principles of this world. Rather, I depend on Christ, who has given me fullness in everything. I am free from all human regulations. My life is with You Christ. You are the head over every power and authority.

Thank You for allowing me to receive You, and thank You for being my salvation . . .

Read:
Genesis 50:20; Luke 10:19

Second Chance

Sovereign God, You Truly Are the God of Second Chances

What the enemy meant for harm, You have turned it for my good! Hallelujah! You have given me authority to trample on snakes and scorpions and to overcome all the power of the enemy. Not one thing will harm me. I do not fear the results of my past failures. You have completely restored me. I have committed all things to You, and You have made me wise. I am now full of joy through the Holy Spirit, and I praise You, Father, Lord of heaven and earth. You are pleased to reveal these things to me. You are honored to reveal Your wisdom to me. I praise You all day long.

Thank You for giving me a second chance . . .

Read:
Psalm 33:15;
1 Corinthians 6:15, 17 & 19–20

You Are Majestic, Adonai

Lord, You have created all mankind. You have formed the hearts of all, and You consider everything we do. I will praise You at all times. My body is a member of Your body. I am drawn to You by love. You have put Your Holy Spirit in me, and I am alive! Praise You, Lord! You have chosen me, and I have chosen You. Therefore, I unite myself with You, and I am one with You in Spirit. I know that I was bought at a price, and I am not my own. I will honor You with my body. You, my Creator, know every detail of my entire body, soul, and mind. It all belongs to You, Jesus. Thank You for giving me understanding. Thank You for pouring out clarity to me.

You are an amazing Creator . . .

Read:
1 Corinthians 12:12–31

The Body

I Praise You for Your Kingdom, Lord

I am a part of the body of Christ. I have been baptized by one Spirit into one body. We have all been given the one Spirit to drink no matter where we came from. God, You have arranged the parts in Your body of believers just the way You want them to be. You have distributed gifts among Your people to make the body complete. We are to use the gifts You have given us for Your glory and honor. We are to be equally concerned for one another. There should be no division among us. We should rejoice with those who rejoice, and suffer with those who suffer. I am Your servant Lord, and I am blessed with Your generous giving of gifts. I will eagerly desire greater gifts from You, Father, so that I may be complete in the body of Christ. Your Kingdom is magnificent.

Thank You for including me in the body . . .

Read:
Luke 10:38–42

Your Presence

Thank You for Your Sweet Presence, Lord

My heart's desire is to sit in Your presence and feel Your love for me, Father. Each time I come and sit at Your feet, I know the filling of Your presence will be greater than the time before. Your desire for me to come to You is actually greater than my own. This opportunity that we have to spend together cannot compare to any other relationship. There is no other task I may have to do that could be more important. It is a sweet and precious time for me to have the privilege to sit in Your presence. I thank You for such favor.

I thank You that I am able to feel Your love in these precious moments we share . . .

Read:
Luke 10:38–42; Acts 10:36; Romans 15:13; 1 Peter 2:25

Peace

God, You Are the Overseer of Peace in My Soul

My emotions, feelings and thoughts are of utmost importance to You. You bring spiritual balance to my entire body through Your Word, through my prayers, and through me choosing to spend time sitting at Your feet. In my obedience, the Holy Spirit is then able to move freely through me and teach me. I am a spiritual being created to worship You, Father. The idea that You are constantly watching over me causes me to want to be perpetually in Your presence where peace is absolute. I am content and at rest knowing You are looking into my heart with Your eyes of grace and mercy. I am thankful. I am at peace in my soul. You fill me with joy and peace as I trust in You so that I may overflow with hope by the power of the Holy Spirit. It is by Your strength that a great balance of peace rests on me.

Thank You, Lord . . .

Read:
1 Corinthians 12:1–11

Spiritual Gifts

Your Spirit is Alive in Me, Jesus

Hallelujah! I am able to say 'Jesus is Lord' through the power of the Holy Spirit. Had it not been for the wonderful work that was done on the cross I would know nothing of this awesome gift. God, You love me too much to let me live my life without Your Spirit abiding inside of me. Not only is Your Spirit living in me, You have also equipped me with spiritual giftings. These sacred endowments are given to me from Your hand. You give gifts through the Spirit, just as You determine. The manifestation of Your Spirit is given to me for the common good. I never want to miss a moment to exercise the talents You have given me. Others will be blessed when I step out in faith and allow You to show me how to utilize these skills. I am obedient to what You are calling me to do. May I acknowledge and put into practice each ability You have imparted to me all the days of my life. Thank You for Your magnificent Spirit that is alive in me.

Thank You for spiritual gifts . . .

Read:
Hebrews 12:14–15

Holiness

You Are Sacred to My Heart, God

I am dedicated to You. You are holy and peaceful. I will make every effort to live in peace with all men and to be holy. Without holiness, I will not see You, Lord. Attaining holiness may seem out of reach, but by Your grace and strength I can have anything You want me to have. I never want to miss out on acknowledging Your grace. Since You have touched me with Your Holy Spirit in a most intimate way, I am sacred to You as well. I am set apart. My name is written in Your book of life. You are taking care of me, and You know everything about me. This relationship is based on trust, love, and truth. I am thankful that I have become so special to You. Thank You that I do not have to strive for holiness. Thank You for accepting me just the way I am. Thank You for Your love, Father.

Thank You for teaching me about holiness . . .

Read:
Psalm 18:2, 10; Ezekiel 37:5; Mark 9:23

Strength

Lord, You Are the Rock That I Run To

You are my Strong Tower. In me there is nothing but emptiness and dry bones, but in You all things come together and are alive. I am humbled by the idea that everything I do is by the power of Your strong hand. I cannot do anything on my own. I acknowledge that every bit of action that I take is because You are a driving force within me that causes great things to happen. Lord, You are sovereign over all things. By You, God, all things are possible. Thank You, Father, for being so strong. Thank You for filling me up with strength, love, ideas and action. Thank You for living inside of me. I am amazed by You! You are my stronghold.

Lord, You are my strength . . .

Read:
Psalm 48; Luke 10:19

Great Are You, Lord, and Most Worthy of Praise

You are so beautiful! You are the citadel I cling to in the raging battle of this world. You have shown Yourself to be my fortress. I am protected by You, God. You are my defense. You preserve and protect the quality and condition of my steps. You are the bastion that guards me as I trample the snakes and scorpions. Nothing will harm me. I will overcome all the power of the enemy. Your right hand is filled with righteousness. Thank You for giving me security forever. Thank You for protecting each step I take.

Thank You for being my beloved guide, even to the end . . .

Read:
Psalm 33:12

Supremacy

You Are the Lord of All Nations, God

The nations are blessed by You. You fully bless the nations who acknowledge You as their Lord. You are supreme! My heart is filled with praise for the One who rules over all the earth. Thank You, Father, for being in control of all things at all times in every nation. You are the ultimate authority in this land, and You are righteous in all Your ways. Thank You for Your supreme leadership.

Thank You for overseeing our world and giving us hope and security in You . . .

Read:
Psalm 139:1; Romans 3:19

Accountability

You Are My Savior, Lord

You are the One that I am accountable to. Glory to Your name, Father! You are most worthy to be praised. I present myself to You each day. Here I am, Lord. I am Yours. The only thing I can bring to You, is myself. I have nothing else to give You but what You have made me to be. I submit my entire being at Your feet. I belong to You, God. Look at who I truly am, and reveal to me things I do not know. Uncover the things I cannot see. With Your help, I can know what I need to change about myself. With Your strengthening power, I will be able to do it. I am thankful You are able to move me in this way. Thank You for answering this prayer for me. Thank You for great revelations.

Thank You for holding me accountable to You, Lord Jesus . . .

Read:
Romans 8:1–4 & 12:9–21

Sincere Love

I Am Serving You, Father

You are the way of love. You have shown me through reading the Bible how to share brotherly love with others. You have taught me what sincere love is and how to honor others above myself. I will never be lacking in zeal, and I will keep my spiritual fervor. I am joyful in hope, patient in affliction, and faithful in prayer. I will be a blessing to those who persecute me, and I will strive to always practice hospitality. You have called me to live in harmony with everyone, and I am willing to associate with all the people in Your creation. I am striving to be careful to do what is right so that Your name may be praised, but I will not be condemned for making mistakes. Thank You for helping me to overcome evil with good.

Thank You for putting a sincere love in my heart for You and for Your people . . .

Read:
Psalm 51:7; Romans 5:9; Ephesians 1:7–8

Your Blood

I Adore You, Abba Father

You were thinking of me when You shed Your blood. You did it willingly and with much love and tenderness. I am validated by You, Holy Father in heaven. You have washed me clean, and I am whiter than snow. I have stability and strength through You, my Lord. Your precious blood has brought justice and liberty to my soul. You have cleansed me in the depths where I thought nothing could ever be reached. I now have redemption through Your blood. I have forgiveness of all my sins in accordance with the riches of Your grace that You lavished on me with all wisdom and understanding. My destiny is confirmed through You, Jesus. I am established because You have verified that I am not guilty. Thank You for this mighty cleansing through Your blood.

Thank You for demonstrating Your love and grace for me through the pouring out of Your pure, innocent blood . . .

Read:
2 Samuel 22:4; Psalm 126:2–3;
Zephaniah 3:17; Hebrews 4:15

Known by You

I Give All My Worship to the One Who Knows My Heart

My praises fall at the feet of the One who created my heart. You are worthy of all my praise, Lord. No one knows me like You, Jesus. You are the creator of man's soul. You know each part of what holds me together. You know where I hurt, and You know what makes me joyful. You sympathize with my pain and weakness, and You delight in my laughter and songs of joy. You are here with me when I feel discouraged, and You provide comfort. You are rejoicing over me with singing. You quiet me with Your love. I am known by You, Lord. Thank You for being a true Father to me. Thank You for accepting my reverent adoration for You.

Thank You for knowing the core of who I really am . . .

Read:
Matthew 5:14, 16; John 3:19–21;
Hebrews 4:13; 1 Peter 2:9

Light

I Lay My Praises Before the Light of the World

You are the light of the world, Lord Jesus. Where there is light, there is no darkness. Darkness flees in Your Holy Presence. Darkness does not have the ability to take away light, yet light, when brought into darkness, can be easily seen by all. Because I live by the truth, I come into the light. Everything I do is done in Your sight. Nothing in all creation is hidden from Your sight, God. Everything is uncovered and laid bare before Your eyes. Your light shines in me because You are in me. I will let my light shine before others so that You may receive all the glory and honor You are due.

Thank You, heavenly Father, for calling me out of darkness into Your wonderful light . . .

Read:
Galatians 3:6–14

Grace

Thank You, Heavenly Father, for Your Grace

Without grace, I would be exhausted from trying to observe the law. Like Abraham, all I have to do is believe You, and I stand before You as righteous. I am justified by You, God, because I have put my faith in You. You have blessed me. I sing Holy is Your name. I am righteous, and I live by faith. I am redeemed from the curse of the law through Christ Jesus, so that by faith I can receive the promise of the Spirit. Amen! What great favor You have shown me Lord! I stand in awe of You, my God and my King. Thank You for Your generosity.

Thank You for grace . . .

Read:
Ephesians 1:3–8

Chosen

O, How I Love You, Jesus

You chose me before the creation of the world to be holy and blameless in Your sight. In love, You predestined me for adoption to sonship through Jesus Christ in accordance with Your pleasure and will to the praise of Your glorious grace which You have freely given me in the One You love. In Jesus, I have redemption through His blood, the forgiveness of sins, in accordance with the riches of Your grace that You lavished on me. I am not fatherless. You are my Father, and I am Your child. I belong to an eternal family with an eternal inheritance. I will pass through this world quickly, but I will remain with You for eternity. Praise be to You, God, the Father of my Lord Jesus Christ, who has blessed me in the heavenly realms with every spiritual blessing in Christ.

Thank You for choosing me, even before creation, to be with You forever . . .

Read:
Psalm 33

Worship

It is Fitting for Me to Sing Joyfully to You Lord

I will always praise Your name. I will shout for joy! I know Your Word is right and true. You are faithful in all You do. Your Word tells me that You love righteousness and justice. Praise You, Father! The earth is full of Your unfailing love. By Your Word the heavens were made and their starry host by the breath of Your mouth. You spoke, and it came to be; You commanded, and it stood firm. Your eyes are on me because I fear You. My hope is in Your unfailing love. I wait in hope for You. You are my help and my shield. My heart rejoices in You. I trust in Your holy name. Thank You for this truth that has enveloped my life. Thank You for allowing me to worship You freely.

Thank You for holding me in Your mighty hand as I worship You . . .

Read:
Luke 11:13; 1 Corinthians 12:4–11; Philippians 4:13

Spiritual Gifts

You Are Strengthening My Belief in You Each Day, Lord My God

I am saved! It is because of my belief in You that I am blessed with spiritual gifts. My faith in You grows stronger each day. The gifts You have placed in me are a reminder of our relationship as child and Father. You freely grant good gifts to Your children, and I am blessed by Your generous heart. I can enjoy these contributions freely lavished on me from the Holy Spirit because I am not bound by any earthly mentality. I am able to do supernatural things through You, Father. You provide strength for me to live. You are living in me, and I continually believe in You. Thank You for saving me, O Righteous One. Thank You for distributing spiritual gifts among Your people.

Thank You for investing in me . . .

Read:
Zephaniah 3:15–19

You Honor Me

I Am on Your Mind, Abba

You are thinking of me day and night. You are with me. You take great delight in me. I do not fear any harm. You have rescued me, and You gathered me to Yourself when I was scattered. You have shown me the depths of Your love in various ways. Like a mother is the only one who can soothe her child with her own love, You use Your love to quiet me and to soothe me. I am humbled in Your arms, where I rest throughout the day. Not just in the morning or at night, but every moment during the day, I am with You, and I am forever on Your mind.

Thank You for the certainty of Your love and honor for me . . .

Read:
Romans 8:28; Revelation 12:11

Overcoming

I Trust You, Father, with All My Circumstances

You have an amazing way of working all things out for my good and for Your purposes. When I look back on all the events of my life, I see Your mighty hand that was at work in each area. I thank You that I have been able to learn from the real life situations I have been through. I am grateful that You have caused me to be a better person because of it all. You are, without a doubt, Sovereign over all things, and I am living proof that You are alive and active. My life is proof that anything can be overcome through You, Father. You are who You say You are. I am pleased and honored to place my life in Your hands. I am overjoyed to trust You in all my ways.

Thank You for being trustworthy, and thank You for helping me to be a victorious overcomer . . .

Read:
Hosea 11:1–4; 1 Corinthians 13:11

Your Presence

Lord, God Almighty, You Are the Same Yesterday and Today and Forever

I praise You for this truth. When I was a child I know You loved me. I know You were with me. I could feel Your holy presence in my life. You called me Your child then, and You still do. Even though I go astray regularly, You continue to love me. You gently call me back to Yourself and protect me from danger. You teach me to walk through this life by tenderly taking me by the arm. You lead me with cords of human kindness and with ties of love. You lift the heavy yoke from my neck and bend down to feed me with Your mighty hand. When I was a child I talked like a child, I thought like a child, I reasoned like a child. When I became an adult I put childish ways behind me. I gain strength and wisdom from spending time with You. I gain understanding and freedom from absorbing Your Word. Thank You for watching over my whole life, God. You have not taken Your eyes off me for one second. Your supervision of me is never-ending.

Thank You for loving me, like a Dad should love his children . . .

Read:
Psalm 139:7; Jeremiah 31:3; Hebrews 4:13;
1 John 3:20; Revelation 22:13

Worship

Master of My World, You Are the Beginning and the End, the Alpha and the Omega, the First and the Last

You hold the entire universe in Your hands, Lord. You see everything that happens. Not one thing is concealed from You, Father. I may try to hide things from others and even from You, yet Your Word tells me that cannot happen. You even see the depths of my soul, and You continue to love me with an everlasting love. You are omniscient – all knowing, omnipresent – everywhere at the same time, and omnipotent – almighty and all powerful. You are a consuming fire that will never let me go. Thank You for caring for me so much in that way. No one and nothing else can compare to Your love for me.

I am forever worshiping Your power
and authority over my life . . .

Read:
Luke 1:68–75

Saved

Praise You, Lord God

You have visited Your people through Your Son, Jesus! You have sent me a Savior! You have redeemed me! The prophets long ago said this would happen, and it did! You are faithful to Your promises. Praise You, Lord! I have been saved! I can now live and walk in freedom! I am not afraid of anyone or anything. You have enabled me to serve You in holiness and righteousness. I will not fear, for You have saved me. The enemy is defeated! I am living victoriously! I will serve You without fear, in holiness and righteousness as long as I live. Thank You for saving me, God Almighty! It feels good to be saved.

Thank You for being my Savior . . .

Read:
Psalm 31:1–5

Refuge

It is Only in You, Lord, That I Take Refuge

You deliver me in Your righteousness. You turn Your ear to me and come quickly to my rescue. You are my Rock of refuge. You are a strong fortress that has saved me. You lead and guide me. You free me from the traps that are set before me. Into Your hands I commit my spirit. You are my Redeemer, O God of truth. I trust fully and completely in You alone. Today is entirely in Your hands, Father. I am so grateful that I can take refuge in the One that has rescued me. What a blessing today is because Your righteousness makes me righteous. I don't have to worry about a thing today. My Father is the God of this universe! You are protecting me, and I am blessed. Thank You Jesus.

Thank You for being my refuge, Lord . . .

Read:
Psalm 51:9–15

Forgiveness

My Tongue Sings of Your Righteousness, O God

When You open my lips, my mouth declares Your praise! You have forgiven all my sin and transgression. You have blotted out my iniquity. Praise You Lord! You have created a pure heart in me. You have renewed a steadfast Spirit within me. You have restored to me the joy of Your salvation. Thank You, Father, for granting me a willing spirit to sustain me. Thank You, Father, for teaching me Your ways. Thank You for the Holy Spirit that lives in me! Thank You for the gift of forgiveness. It feels good to be free from guilt.

It feels good to be clean . . .

Read:
Mark 12:30–31; 2 John 6

Love

You Are Love, Father

You created love, and You created me to love You. I am trying each day to follow through with Your commandments. I know that Your desire is that I love You first and then love my neighbor as myself. Teach me to walk in love each day, Father. I am to walk in obedience to Your commands. I am to walk in love. Thank You for giving me the ability to love Your creation, Your children, and most importantly, You. I am overjoyed at the thought of being able to love. Thank You for creating love within me.

Only You could do such a marvelous thing in a person, Lord . . .

Read:
James 4:10

Worship

I Am Here to Worship You, Father

I bow down at Your feet. You are a perfect picture of holiness to me. It brings me great joy and humility to bow before You, Lord. I feel as though I am where I need to be when I put my face to the ground before You. This is one of my acts of worship to You. I am indeed lifted up when I am in this position. It is the highest place Your majesty can take me. Thank You for making this supernatural meeting place available for us.

Thank You for granting me times to worship You . . .

Read:
Romans 14:1–12

Stand

Thank You and Praise You, Jesus, for Making Me Able to Stand

I admit that I am weak, and I am in need of help. I am so thankful that You accept me, Lord. We are all made different, and we all have different matters. I will not pass judgment on another man's faith. Everything I do is unto You, Lord. I belong to You, no matter my circumstances. You are my Lord. We will all stand before Your judgment seat and bow before You. I will give an account of myself to You, Father. May I keep my lips from passing judgment on another, and may I pray for those in need. In doing so, I will be able to stand in the posture that points others toward You. Thank You for accepting me just as I am, Lord. Thank You for helping me in my weaknesses.

Thank You for enabling me to stand . . .

Read:
Numbers 6:26; Psalm 34:14; Isaiah 9:6; Zechariah 9:9–10; 1 Thessalonians 4:11

Peace

Jesus, You Are the Everlasting Father and the Prince of Peace

You have granted Your people peace. You have taught us to seek peace and pursue it. I rejoice greatly in You, Lord. You came to me righteous and having salvation, gentle and riding on a donkey. You take away wars and battles and proclaim peace to the nations. Your rule extends from sea to sea and from the river to the ends of the earth. Thank You for giving us peace in our hearts and souls. Thank You for coming to us and giving Yourself up for us so that we can live quiet peaceable lives through You.

Thank You for granting us peace . . .

Read:
Isaiah 42:5–6; Isaiah 43:15; 1 Peter 4:19

Called

You Are My Creator

You are unlike me... not created, but *the* Creator! You are my Holy One! You are my King! You created the heavens and stretched them out. You spread out the earth with all that springs from it. You give breath to Your people and life to all those who walk upon the earth You created. You call me into righteousness. You take hold of my hand. I commit myself to You, Lord. I will continue to do good. It may very well feel like suffering at times, but You have promised me a life eternal with You in Glory. Thank You for remaining faithful and true to me. Thank You for giving me each breath I take.

Thank You for calling me toward righteousness because You love me . . .

Read:
Psalm 103:5; Jeremiah 31:3

Relationship

I Cheerfully Welcome You Today with My Praise, Dear Father

You alone are worthy to be praised. This is an outstanding relationship we have. You are my deep desire. You are Holy. You are the Giver of life. What was once dead has now come to life. What was once in ruin is now standing firm on the rock of my Salvation. Praise be to the God who satisfies my desires with good things so that my youth is renewed like the eagle's. I am Your beloved, and You love me with an everlasting love. I know that I belong to You. Thank You for loving me, Abba. Thank You for bringing me into this relationship with You.

Thank You for being an approachable and desirable God and Father . . .

Read:
Deuteronomy 32:4;
Matthew 5:48; Ecclesiastes 3:1

Victory

You Are Perfect in All Your Ways, Father

You have perfectly won the victory. You have appointed a time and a season for every activity under heaven. I take joy in knowing that by You and through You all things are working. You are the One who shall receive glory for all things. Sometimes it seems as though my life is spinning out of control. That is when it is imperative that I remember *who* is in control of all things. The battle is already won. I must keep in mind that death has been defeated by Your resurrection! I must look to the cross when I feel defenseless and see that it is empty, and You are victorious! Thank You for Your Word that has taught me how to overcome the feeling of defeat. It is because of this triumphal victory that I can know that You are in control of all things that happen under the sun. Thank You for the conflict override.

Thank You for granting me a free win . . .

Read:
Colossians 1:15–17

Creation

Lord, You Are Over Everything

Jesus, You are the image of the invisible God, the firstborn over all creation. I give You praise! By You, all things were created: things in heaven and on earth, visible and invisible, whether thrones or powers or rulers or authorities. All things were created by You and for You. You are before all things, and in You all things hold together. You hold me together, Lord, everyday. I cannot even walk without You holding me up. My strength comes solely and completely from You. I am weak, and You are strong for me in every way. Jesus, You are my everything. You are all that is good. Everything made by Your hands is under Your care.

Thank You for Your creation . . .

Read:
1 Corinthians 1:4–9

Fellowship

I Praise You for Our Time of Fellowship Now and Forevermore, Lord

You have enriched me in every way by the grace You have abundantly given me. I do not lack any spiritual gift. I wait eagerly for You to be revealed. You are keeping me strong during this time. It is by Your strength that I will be able to remain firm through this journey of life to the end. And on that day, You will look upon me as Your child. You will reclaim me, and I will be blameless. I will be Yours forever. You have called me into fellowship with You, and You are faithful to our relationship. Thank You for enriching me with grace and strength throughout my days.

Thank You for our fellowship and for my hope in You . . .

Read:
Psalm 105:1–5

Remembrance

Lord I Give You Thanks, and I Call on Your Wonderful Name

I proclaim to others the numerous things You have done for me. I sing to You. I sing many praises to Your name each day. You have done many wonderful works. I glory in Your holy name. May my heart rejoice proudly because I am seeking You, Lord. I will always look to You, Lord. I will look to You for strength, and I will ever seek Your face. I will always remember the things You have done for me. I will never forget the many wonders and miracles I have seen by Your mighty hand. I will remember all the mercy You have shown me throughout my days. You are my Lord. You are my God. You deserve the highest praise. Thank You for being my Savior.

May I always remember to praise my Father in heaven . . .

Read:
Romans 12:3–8

Gifted

I Honor You, Father, with Who I Am

I am gifted according to the grace You have given me, Jesus. It is Your will for me to use my gifts for Your glory and honor. I do not think of myself higher than I should, but I look upon myself with sober judgment, in accordance with the measure of faith You have distributed to me. I have one body with many members that all have different functions. In the same way, we who are in Christ are many members that form one body. Each of us belong to one another in Christ. You have given us spiritual giftings, such as prophesy, serving, teaching, encouraging, giving generously, diligent leadership and showing mercy. Thank You for letting us be a part of such an amazing body held together by Your precious hands.

Thank You for gifting us . . .

Read:
Proverbs 3:1–2; 1 Corinthians 1:20, 30

Wisdom

In You, God, is All Wisdom

Keen perception comes from knowing Your Word. I will keep Your commands in my heart, for they will prolong my life many years. I will not forget Your teachings. You will bring prosperity for my remembrance and obedience. Not one thing can compare to Your infinite wisdom. My human nature wants to seek wisdom from this world, however, You are so faithful, Father, to gently remind me that You sent Jesus to me so that I may know You through Him. Christ Jesus is my wisdom from You, God, that is my righteousness, holiness and redemption. And I say You, God, have made foolish the wisdom of the world. Your wisdom causes me to believe.

I thank You that Your Word, as well as Your Spirit, is the source of wisdom for me . . .

Read:
1 Corinthians 13:1–3

Love

God, You Are Love, and You Have Shown Me Love

You have taught me how to love. Your Word advances my knowledge of love. I desire to love as You have loved me. If I speak in the tongues of men and of angels, but have not love, I am only a resounding gong or a clanging cymbal. If I have the gift of prophesy and can fathom all mysteries and all knowledge, and if I have a faith that can move mountains, but have not love, I am nothing. If I give all I possess to the poor and surrender my body to the flames, but have not love, I gain nothing. My deepest need is to love others as You love them, Jesus. I know about love, I have been loved, and You are teaching me how to love every day. I am putting my love into action today. I will love as You have loved me. I will love when no one else will. I am love because You are love, and Your Spirit is alive in me. Thank You, Jesus!

Thank You for showing me love and for showing me how to love . . .

Read:
John 4:23–24

Worship

Lord, You Are the Savior of the World

You are Spirit, God. I am a worshipper. I will worship You in spirit and in truth. I want to be the kind of true worshiper that You seek. When I choose to stay in fellowship with You throughout the day, I am worshiping You. My time with You is sacred. I want my entire day to be filled with Your presence. The only way I can achieve this is if I stay in the spirit of worship toward You all day long. Your presence makes my day easier. Things tend to run more smoothly when I allow Your presence to permeate through me. The stresses of a normal day melt away when I keep my posture turned toward You, Father. I choose to worship You, God, in spirit and in truth. Thank You for allowing me the privilege to honor You through these actions.

Thank You for the gift of worship . . .

Read:
Psalm 31:7–9, 14–16

Love

I Am Glad Today, Father

I rejoice in Your love. Yes, there is trouble all around me, but I serve an almighty, powerful God! You, Father, have seen my afflictions, and You have been merciful to me. Sometimes it seems as though my strength fails and my bones grow weak, yet You are always there to pick me up and set my feet in a spacious place. I stand on Christ, the solid Rock. I trust in You, Lord. You are my God. All of my times are in Your hands, O sovereign God of heaven. Your face shines on me, and You save me and consume me with Your unfailing love. Your love is the reason I exist. Thank You for Your love, God. Thank You for seeing me and helping me. Thank You for Your Word that encourages me and pierces my heart with love.

I bless You, Lord, my God . . .

Read:
Proverbs 4:1–7

Wisdom

All Wisdom is From You, Father

Lord, You are wisdom. You are understanding. You give the ultimate instruction. You give me sound learning. I gain all my knowledge from Your teaching. There is no other who has the authority to fill my mind with anything. My mind belongs to You, Holy One. I lay hold of Your words with my heart. I will keep Your commands and live. I will not forget Your words or swerve from them. Your wisdom protects me in my way. I love Your supreme wisdom. Thank You for making wisdom available to me. Thank You for instructing me to embrace Your wisdom. Thank You for allowing me to gain the understanding that this is the best way for me to live.

Thank You for sharing Your wisdom with me, my Teacher . . .

Read:
2 Thessalonians 2:13–17

Chosen

You Chose Me from the Beginning

I love You so much, God. You chose me to be saved through the sanctifying work of the Spirit and through belief in the truth. What a privilege it is for me to be called to this by You through the gospel of Jesus Christ. I thank You for the eternal encouragement and good hope You have given to my heart. Thank You for this strengthening that takes place in my life as I walk with You daily. I am standing firm and holding to Your truth. Thank You for being my God and Father.

I am so thankful to know I am loved
and chosen by You, Lord . . .

Read:
Mark 1:8

Holy Spirit

I Am Baptized by Your Holy Spirit, Father

I believe in You, God. I am saved! I carry Your Spirit with me wherever I may go. The Holy Spirit lives inside of my soul, and I represent You, Christ. As a Christian, I strive to exemplify Your character proudly. So with much prayer, fasting, and time spent in Your Word, I gain the strength and tools needed to attain my goals. Thank You for equipping me each day as we commune together. Thank You for choosing to reside in me.

Thank You for pouring out Your Spirit onto me so that I can portray the authenticity of the One true God . . .

Read:
1 Peter 1:3–6

Living Hope

Praise Be to You, Yahweh, the God and Father of Our Lord Jesus Christ

You have given me new birth into a living hope through the resurrection of Jesus Christ. You are making a way for me through the sufferings and trials. I realize this grief is just temporary. It is in Your great mercy that I will walk into an inheritance that can never perish, spoil or fade. You have a place in heaven for me. I greatly rejoice in the faith You have provided for me. You are shielding me with Your power until the coming of the salvation that is ready to be revealed in the last time. Thank You for carrying me through.

Thank You for this living hope I have in You, Christ Jesus . . .

Read:
Psalm 133:1; Ephesians 4:2–13

Unity

Unity is from You, Father of All Things

You are the One God and Father of all creation. You are the great Creator of unity. I come to know You better by uniting together with the Spirit through the bond of peace. You have filled the whole universe with Your Holy Spirit so that the body of Christ can be built up and achieve unity in the faith. May we be a completely humble people. May we be gentle and patient, bearing with one another in love. How good and pleasant it is when brothers live together in unity. Thank You for making us one in the bond of love. Thank You for uniting us together with Yourself so that You could graciously unite us together with one another.

Thank You for unity in the faith, Jesus . . .

Read:
Isaiah 42:8; 1 Corinthians 15:58;
2 Corinthians 4:17

Power and Glory

You Are the Lord

You will not yield Your glory to another. You are the Lord of Lords. I honor the Maker of the entire existence of all things. Nothing is left out or held back from You, Father. You are aware of each trouble that takes place in my life. Although I may feel hard pressed on every side, I am not crushed. I might feel perplexed, but I am not in despair. I know in this life I will be persecuted, but I am not abandoned. Yes, at times I will feel struck down, but I am not destroyed! I will stand firm! I will let nothing move me. I will always give myself fully to the work of You, Lord! I know that my labor in You is not in vain. You are my reward, Lord Jesus! My light and momentary troubles are achieving for me an eternal glory that far outweighs them all. Thank You for being my Lord! Thank You for Your glory!

Thank You for Your unlimited power and glory that comes alive in my life . . .

Read:
Matthew 14:29; Colossians 2:2

Savior

Praise You, Savior in Heaven and Here on Earth

You, Lord, have made me whole. The mystery of Your love overwhelms me. My heart is encouraged by You, and we are united in love. I am consumed by Your glory. You are my redeemer. When I was down, You lifted me up. You lifted my head so that I could set my eyes upon You. You gathered together every part of my being and made me whole and complete. You made my faith strong in Your presence. I am walking on the water, as my eyes are focused on You. You are dedicated to ensuring that I may have the full riches of complete understanding. My soul thirsts for You, my Savior, and You, O Lord, fill me up to overflowing. Thank You for Your saving grace.

Thank You for being my Savior . . .

Read:
Psalm 18

Praise

I Praise You, Exalted One

In my distress I call to You, Lord. I cry to You for help. From Your temple You hear my voice. My cry comes before You into Your ears. You bring me out into a spacious place. You rescue me because You delight in me. God, Your ways are perfect. Your Word is flawless. You are a shield for me because I have chosen to take refuge in You. You are my Lord, my Rock and my God. You arm me with strength and make my way perfect. You make my feet like the feet of a deer. You enable me to stand on the heights. You train my hands for battle; my arms can bend a bow of bronze. You give me Your shield of victory and Your right hand sustains me. You stoop down to make me great. You are alive, Lord! Praise be to my Rock!

You are exalted, my Savior . . .

Read:
Colossians 3:1–10

New Life

O Praise You, Father in Heaven

I have been raised with You, Christ. My heart is set on things above, not on earthly things. I have died and my life is now hidden with You, in God. I am not my own. When You appear, I will also appear with You in Glory. You have put to death the things that were in me that belong to the earthly nature. I have taken off my old self with its practices, and I have put on the new self, which is being renewed in knowledge, in the image of my Creator.

Thank You for giving me new life in You . . .

Read:
Ephesians 6:10–13

Armor

Lord, You Are My God and My Savior

You are gracious and powerful. All things are protected by Your mighty hand. I will be strong in You and in Your mighty power. By putting on the armor You have provided for me, I can take my stand against the devil's schemes. I understand that my struggle is not against flesh and blood, but against the rulers, against the authorities, against the powers of this dark world and against the spiritual forces of evil in the heavenly realms. Therefore, I will put on the full armor of God so that when the day of evil comes I will be able to stand my ground, and after I have done everything, I will stand. This powerful armor You have rendered, defends me and makes me strong. Thank You for providing such dynamic protection for me in this world. I can do all things with You.

Thank You for armor, Lord God . . .

Read:
Psalm 106

Praise

Praise You, Lord

I give thanks to You, Lord, for You are good. Your love endures forever. Thank You for remembering me when You show favor to Your people. Thank You for coming to my aid. Thank You for saving me. You did all this so that I may enjoy the prosperity of Your chosen ones. I may share in the joy of Your nation and join Your inheritance in giving praise. Even though I am a sinner and have done many wrong things, You continue to love me and show Your kindness to me. I will give thanks to You for all Your holiness and for all the grace that has been given to me through Your righteous right hand. Glory to You, God.

Praise be to the Lord from everlasting to everlasting . . .

Read:
Romans 12:1–2

Spiritual Gifts

Praise Be to the Giver of Every Good Gift

I am spiritually gifted by You, Father. You have transformed me by renewing my mind. I do not conform to the pattern of this world. I offer my body as a living sacrifice to You. My body is holy and pleasing to You when I do this. It is my spiritual act of worship to You, my King. I am able to test and approve what Your will is because I have humbled myself and presented myself to You in the way You have taught me through Your Word. Your good, pleasing and perfect will is my desire, and I will pursue it all the days of my life. I will use the spiritual tools You have equipped me with. Thank You for transforming me.

Thank You for gifting me . . .

Read:
Psalm 37:4; Matthew 11:28–29; James 4:8

Your Presence

Lord, Where You Are is Where I Want to Be

I have a burning desire to stay close to You, Abba Father. In Your presence is the sweetest place I have ever been. I love it when Your Spirit surrounds me. I feel comfort, love, joy and peace when I am near to Your heart, Father. Never before have I ever been enveloped with the quiet rest You give to me when I come to You in the secret place. Thank You for honoring me by surrounding me with Your Holy presence. Thank You for giving me the desires of my heart.

Thank You for meeting with me each day . . .

Read:
Psalm 10:17; Hebrews 3:13; Hebrews 10:25

Encouragement

You Are My Great Encourager, Lord Jesus

You have created a multitude of positive attitudes in the depths of my being. I have become increasingly dependent upon Your encouragement to make it through each day. It is Your faithfulness to speak to me and inspire me that causes me to be an encouragement to others. I have been blessed to glean wisdom from the One who offers and gives it so freely. We advance further together each day as we commune with one another. Your stimulating, penetration to my heart induces support to my spirit. Each endeavor brings a new uplifting feeling to my spirit as long as I allow You full control. I know You are with me. You have a place in my soul in which You communicate love to me each time I sit quietly in Your presence. This is a great encouragement to me. This is how I know You are real.

Thank You for Your loving kindness that encourages me . . .

Read:
Psalm 31:19–24; Isaiah 40:31; John 16:33

Hope

Praise Be to the God of Hope

I love You Lord! My hope is in You, Father. How great is Your goodness, which You have stored up for those who fear You. You bestow Your goodness in the sight of men on those who take refuge in You. I take refuge in You, God. I dwell in the shelter of Your presence. You hide me in Your place and keep me safe from the things of this world. You have shown Your wonderful love to me, and I praise You for it. You hear my cry for mercy when I am in need of Your help. You have preserved me because You love me. I am strong, and I will take heart. All my hope is in You, Lord. Thank You for giving me hope in hopeless times. Thank You for hearing my cry. Thank You for Your goodness to me. Thank You for Your faithfulness. Thank You for giving me great things to look forward to.

Thank You for hope . . .

Read:
Proverbs 4:8–13

Wisdom

Jesus, You Are So Wise

You amaze me with Your wisdom. You are gentle in giving me intellectual integrity. I have esteemed Your wisdom, and I am exalted by it. Your words honor me as I am obedient. Your wisdom has set a garland of grace on my head and presented me with a crown of splendor. How precious are the words of Your lips as they fall on me. You guide me in the way of wisdom and lead me along straight paths. My steps are not hampered as I walk, gracious Father. When I run, I do not stumble. I hold on to Your instruction. I will not let it go. I guard this gift well, for it is my life. Thank You for permission to take hold of such mature understanding. I worship You, Jesus.

Praise to You, my Lord . . .

Read:
Jude 20–21

Eternal Life

Thank You, God, for Giving Me Eternal Life Through Your Son, Jesus Christ

I praise and worship the One who paid my debt. I am thankful that You saw me and saved me. You have placed a most holy faith within me that builds me up and preserves me for eternity. I will keep myself in Your love as I wait for Your mercy to bring me to eternal life. I will continue to pray in the Holy Spirit and receive the love You have for me each day. Thank You for this divine gift of Your presence within me.

Thank You for eternal life . . .

Read:
Hebrews 6:18–20

Hope

You Give Me Hope, God

You are greater than any man. You are the greatest of all. You are perfect, and You are flawless. You have made Your promises clear to me. I take hold of the hope set before me, and I am greatly encouraged. Hope is an anchor for my soul. I stand firm and secure in Your presence. I thank You, Jesus, for being my forerunner. You entered the inner sanctuary behind the curtain on my behalf and became my high priest forever. Thank You for this soul-firming truth. My feet are planted solid in this life because of this hope You have situated deep in my soul.

My hope is in You, Father . . .

Read:
Psalm 119:89–104

Eternal Word

Your Word is Eternal, Lord

Your Word stands firm in the heavens. You are faithful through all the generations. You established the earth, and it endures. Your Word is my delight, and I live by it. You have consecrated my life by teaching me to follow Your ways. Your commands are boundless, and I cling to them. I will meditate on and ponder the good words contained in my Bible. This is where I gain wisdom and insight. I will obey Your Word, and I will not depart from it. You, Yourself, have taught me the secret things in the secret place. How sweet are Your words to my taste, sweeter than honey to my mouth. Thank You for Your everlasting Word that has stood up through all generations.

Thank You for helping me to live by Your eternal Word every day . . .

Read:
Isaiah 26:3; Matthew 22:37; Romans 12:2

Mind

You Are Worthy of My Praise, Lord Jesus

You have my mind's full attention, and my praises and worship are for You. I love You with all of my mind. With so many worldly things pulling at my mind, I am determined to keep You in the forefront. You are of greatest importance to me. I have the mind of Christ. I want my every thought to be clinging to Your truth. I trust in You, and You are keeping me in perfect peace because my mind is steadfast. I will not be swayed or moved. You have captivated me, and I am staying here with You. Thank You for capturing my attention, Lord.

Thank You for transforming me by renewing my mind . . .

Read:
2 Peter 3:9–18

Looking Forward

I Look Forward To Your Appearing

To You, my Lord and Savior, Jesus Christ, be glory, both now and forevermore. I am keeping with Your promise that I will see a new heaven and a new earth, the home of righteousness. You have given me wisdom and salvation. You are not slow in keeping Your promises to me. You are patient with me and all Your children. It is not Your desire that anyone should perish, but that everyone come to repentance. Let us make every effort to be found spotless, blameless, and at peace with You, Father. Thank You for being so gracious and patient with Your children. Thank You for giving us the promise of heaven.

Thank You for giving us an everlasting life with our King to look forward to . . .

Read:
Isaiah 61:1–3

Deliverance

Your Spirit, Sovereign Lord, is on Me

You have anointed me to preach the good news to the poor. You have sent me to bind up the brokenhearted, to proclaim freedom for the captives, and release the prisoners from darkness. Lord, You have bound up my broken heart. You have set this captive free, released this prisoner from darkness, and Your favor rests on me. You have been faithful to comfort me when I have mourned, and You have provided for me when I have grieved. You bestow on me a crown of beauty instead of ashes, the oil of gladness instead of mourning, and a garment of praise instead of a spirit of despair. You call me an oak of righteousness, planted by Your hands for the display of Your splendor.

Thank You, Jesus, for delivering me . . .

Read:
Psalm 135:1–5; Philippians 2:9–11

Treasured Possession

I Am Your Treasured Possession

Lord, You have chosen me to be Your own. You are a good God, and I sing praises to Your name. I am fully aware that this is pleasing to You. You are greater than any other. You are higher than any mountain. You are King of Kings and Lord of Lords. You are mighty to save. You are exalted among the nations. You are the Creator and Ruler of the entire universe. At Your name, every knee will bow in heaven and on earth and under the earth, and every tongue will confess that You, Jesus Christ, are Lord, to the glory of God the Father, yet You have chosen me to be Your very own. You have chosen me to be Your treasured possession. How I love You, Jesus.

I thank You that I am of great importance and value to You, Lord . . .

Read:
Colossians 4:2–6; 1 Peter 3:15

Prayer

I Am Devoted to Prayer

Hallelujah to You, God, for allowing me to pray. I am watchful and thankful. I look for opportunities to proclaim the mystery of Christ. You open doors for Your message to go forth. I will proclaim Your message clearly and precisely, as the Holy Spirit guides. Through prayer You give me Your wisdom so that I will know the things to say to those who do not know You. I will make the most of every opportunity. I will let my conversation always be full of grace and seasoned with salt so that I may know how to answer people. You have prepared me to give an answer to everyone who asks me to give the reason for the hope I have. I will do it with gentleness and respect. Thank You, Father, for teaching me through Your Word and through prayer. Thank You for equipping me.

Thank You for prayer . . .

Read:
Romans 8:28

Balance

I Worship You in All Your Glory, Dear Father

You bring such balance to my life, God. You can see everything on a larger scale. It is all clear and accurate to You, Holy God. Your loving hands have distributed all things in perfect proportion. I am able to see touches of beauty that can come only from my Creator. You are awesome in all Your splendor, dear Jesus. You administer equal parts of Your glory to every aspect of my world. At the end of the day, I am blessed to see how You have shown up in each area that needed Your attention. I thank You for open eyes so that I may see how You make each entity come together with such grace.

I thank You for creating balance . . .

Read:
Psalm 16

O Holy Father, it is You Who Keeps Me Protected

You are my place of safety, and I take refuge in You. Apart from You, I have no good thing. You assign me my portion and make me secure. The boundary lines have fallen for me in pleasant places because of You, Father. I know that my inheritance will be delightful. You will always go up ahead of me and prepare things for me. You are faithful to counsel me. I do not fear abandonment, and I will never be shaken. I know You, Lord, and You are carrying me through all things and making my path of life secure. My heart is glad. My tongue rejoices. My body and mind will rest peacefully protected by You. I am overwhelmed at Your holy shield on my life.

Thank You for this kind of protection,
sweet heavenly Father . . .

Read:
Proverbs 18:10

Strength

Your Name is a Strong Tower, Lord

The righteous run to it and are safe. Such comfort I find in running to You, Jesus. You are the only refuge that offers shelter and peace from life's difficulties and worries. I am protected by Your mighty hand in all I do, and I am safe in Your arms. I will not worry or fear what is to come because You give me assurance that You will take care of it all. I know I am secure when I choose to run to the Strong Tower that is waiting for me each day. Your strength will be my strength. I will acknowledge this truth all day long.

Thank You, Holy Father, for being the strength of the strong . . .

Read:
Isaiah 26:3; Matthew 6:33–34;
Philippians 4:13

Overcoming

I Declare That You, Father, Are the God of This Day

All things will answer to You today. Each day brings a new set of challenges. Most of these frivolous situations strive to fill up my mind and try to replace You. However, You have given me wisdom, Father, to allow You to be first in all I do. It is my responsibility to recognize when something is competing for my time with You. I am to manage the circumstance accordingly with help from You. I choose You over the trivial conditions this world offers. When I am in Your presence, I can accomplish all things. Thank You for being the Lord of my mind.

Thank You for giving me another day of victory . . .

Read:
1 Timothy 3:16

Your Presence

I Eagerly Desire You, Jesus

I am all about being in Your presence. I long to see miraculous signs and wonders straight from You, Holy God. My interest is not in the same old, same old mundane daily routines of this world. I want to see You! The deep mystery of You living inside of me is unfathomable to my feeble mind, yet this truth has been displayed in Your people for over two-thousand years. I am convinced that You are real, active and alive inside of me. I know this because I feel Your Spirit of truth walking with me throughout each day. When You display Your presence in my everyday situations, my desire for You deepens. My eyes are turned toward You. The eyes of my heart become open, and our relationship increases in love, faith, hope and security. Thank You for giving me the desire to desire You, Jesus.

Thank You for fulfilling my passions of wanting to be with You . . .

Read:
Proverbs 1:2–7

Wisdom

Lord, God, You Hold All the Wisdom I Long For

Your Word is packed with truth and understanding for me to embrace. When I take moments throughout the day to read Your infallible Word, I am disciplining myself for attaining wisdom. This is a gift You have provided for those who love You and fear You. I want to do what is right and just and fair. I want to live a prudent and disciplined life. Your Word is where I gain my knowledge and discretion. I will listen to Your Word and add to my learning. I am blessed by the guidance Your Word provides. Thank You, Father, for giving me wisdom through Your Word.

I thank You that wisdom is available to me for gaining understanding directly from You . . .

Read:
Psalm 145:5, 10–12

Glory of God

You Are Glorious, Lord

You are completely enjoyable! The fullness of Your glory is brilliant. I am delighted to set my eyes on Your magnificent splendor. I will speak of the glorious splendor of Your majesty. I will meditate on Your wonderful works. All things that You have made will praise You, Lord. I will tell of the glory of Your Kingdom. I see all the blessings You have bestowed upon Your world. They are many. I thank You, God, for providing me opportunities each day to enjoy the things You have set before me. May I never miss a moment to praise Your mighty works. I will take time out of each day to acknowledge Your great works and wonders.

Thank You for allowing me to enjoy the glorious riches and excellence of Your Kingdom . . .

Read:
Numbers 6:24–27

Blessings

You Are My Blessing, Lord

You are the One thing that blesses me. I am completely blessed and kept by You, God. You have caused Your face to shine upon me. You are incredibly gracious to me in countless ways. You turn Your face toward me and give me peace. Your name is written on my soul forever. Thank You for blessing me with more than I deserve. Thank You for being so gracious and loving. You have shown me this blessing through Your written Word.

I am Yours, Lord, and You are mine . . .

Read:
2 Chronicles 20:5–30; Psalm 24:8

Victory

You Are the King of Glory and Victory, God

You are strong and mighty in my battles. I cannot fight in my own strength. It was You who won all the victories for Your people in Your Word. They gave You praises and acknowledged that power and might are in Your hand, and no one can withstand You. They did not know what to do, but their eyes were upon You. That is my prayer for this day I am living in. I will praise You as I go into battle, and I will praise You as I am coming out. I may not know what to do, but my eyes are on You, Jesus. You are the Victor! I give thanks to You, Lord.

My life is at peace, for You, my God, have given me rest on every side . . .

Read:
Deuteronomy 32:4; 2 Samuel 22:31;
Matthew 5:48; Hebrews 10:14

Perfection

All Your Ways Are Perfect, Lord Jesus

You are complete, and I am complete in You, Father. I lack nothing when I am in Your presence because Your fullness envelopes my soul. You are excellent in all Your ways. You are supreme. At times, I tend to feel inadequate, hurt, incomplete and broken, yet when I simply come into Your presence, worship and repent, I become clean, pure, full and renewed. This kind of love is mind-blowing to a fleshly vessel as myself. I stand in awe of You, Lord. Thank You for absolute wholeness and beauty that You restore to me so freely, as I come to You with my face to the ground.

Thank You for making me complete and perfect in Your Holy presence . . .

Read:
John 1:17; Romans 5:17; Romans 11:5–6

Grace

Today, I Worship My Savior of Grace

You have given me abundant provisions of grace and the gift of righteousness through Jesus Christ. You did not approve of me by my works. I have been chosen by Your grace. I can only understand this overwhelming gift through Your wisdom and the Holy Spirit. Even then, I still find it hard to believe that You just love me that much. Your grace is incredible. I cannot get over it. You have warmed my heart with this precious gift, and I am going to praise You all the days of my life. I will celebrate You, Lord. You have made me glad. I am hand selected by my Father to receive grace. Thank You for choosing me by Your grace, Jesus.

Thank You for giving me grace every single day of my life . . .

Read:
Philippians 3:12–15; Hebrews 13:8

Hope

My Father, You Are Unlimited and Boundless

You are infinite and immeasurable. You are the same yesterday and today and forever. What an awesome promise of hope for Your people! I cling to Your promises. Yes! I press on to take hold of that for which Christ Jesus took hold of me. I forget what is behind me and strain toward what is ahead. I press on toward the goal to win the prize for which God has called me heavenward in Christ Jesus. Thank You, God, for making these things clear to me. You are my helper, and You have cleared the way for me. Thank You for making it easy for me to soar into eternity. Thank You for Your infinite love today, yesterday and forever. Thank You for helping me press on toward the goal. Thank You for sharing heaven with me.

Thank You for giving me great and everlasting hope . . .

Read:
Psalm 95:1, 6–7; Psalm 139:1; Jeremiah 1:5

Worship

My Savior, My King, You Are Holy, Holy, Holy

I love You. I worship You. You are my God and my King. You bear my burdens. Thank You, Jesus. I bow down in Your presence and worship You. I kneel before my Maker. I am under Your care. I acknowledge that You are God, and there is no other. You are good in all Your ways. My heart sings with great joy and gratitude for Your goodness to me. I am called by You. You have searched me, Lord. You know me in every way, better than I know myself. Before I was born, You set me apart to worship You. Thank You for knowing who I truly am, Lord.

Thank You for being available so that I may worship You . . .

Read:
Ephesians 2:10, Philippians 1:6

Complete

I Am Complete in You, Jesus

I praise You for completing who I am through Yourself. I am Your workmanship, created in Christ Jesus to do good works, which You prepared in advance for me to do. I know I am not required to perform a certain way to be pleasing to You. You see all my imperfections, and You love me anyway. As I walk in Your Spirit, my heart longs to be like You, Jesus. I read in Your word that You showed love to everyone You encountered. I am eager to love others and show the love of Christ through the things I do and the words I say. You have begun a good work in me, and I know You will carry it on to completion until the day of Christ Jesus. Thank You for this promise.

Thank You for completing me . . .

Read:
Colossians 3:12–17

Chosen

I Am Chosen By You, Lord Jesus

I praise the Father, the Son and the Holy Spirit. I am holy and dearly loved by You. You have clothed me with compassion, kindness, humility, gentleness and patience. Your love and the love You placed in me, binds all these virtues together in perfect unity. I am thankful for Your peace that rules in my heart. Your Word dwells in me richly. I will teach and admonish others with the wisdom You have granted me. I will do it all in the name of Jesus, who raised me up and set my heart on things above. Thank You for this life, Lord.

Thank You for choosing me, and thank You for loving me . . .

Read:
Ephesians 6:14–18

Armor

I Praise You, Powerful Father in Heaven

I am Your soldier. My armor is in place today. You have provided, and I am partaking in this gift of protection and love. I stand firm with my belt of truth buckled around my waist, with my breastplate of righteousness in place, and with my feet fitted with the readiness that comes from the gospel of peace. In addition to all this, I take up my shield of faith, with which I can extinguish all the flaming arrows of the evil one. I take my helmet of salvation and my sword of the Spirit, which is the Word of God. I pray in the Spirit on all occasions with all kinds of prayers and requests. With this in mind, I am alert, and I always keep on praying for all the saints. You are my guide who goes before me in all my endeavors. My hope is in You, Father. Thank You for Your provision and for Your protection.

Thank You for providing armor for Your Christian soldiers . . .

Read:
Psalm 5

Prayer

Jehovah Shammah, You Know My Heart and Every Thought in My Mind

O Lord, I know You hear the words from my mouth even before they leave my lips. You listen to my cries and hear my voice when I pray to You. I lay my prayers before You in the morning, and I wait in reverent expectation. I am able to come into Your presence anytime throughout my day and bow down to You. You lead me in Your righteousness so that I can take my stand against evil. I take refuge in You, and it makes me glad and joyful. You have spread Your protection over me and enclosed me with Your favor. You are a shield of love surrounding me with blessings. All this is available through my choosing to open my heart to You through prayer and belief. Thank You for Your help and protection. Thank You for Your love.

Thank You for the precious gift of prayer . . .

Read:
1 Corinthians 1:25–31

Wisdom

You Have Supreme Wisdom, Lord

Your wisdom surpasses all. In fact, the foolishness of You, God, is wiser than any human wisdom. When I begin to think that I am wise in my own eyes, I am gently reminded that all wisdom comes from You. I will not boast. It is because of You that I am in Christ Jesus, who has become wisdom for me from You, God – that is, my righteousness, holiness and redemption. Therefore, if I am going to boast about anything, I will boast in You, Lord. May You receive the honor and glory due to You.

Thank You for generously imparting a modest portion of Your wisdom to me . . .

Read:
Genesis 1:27; Psalm 111; Ecclesiastes 5:7

Your Creation

I Was Created to Praise You, Lord

You are an absolute essential part of my life, Father. Apart from You, I can do nothing. In You alone, there is life. You created me for Yourself. I cannot keep from praising You. My whole heart is linked to You. I was created in Your image. Great are Your works, Lord. Glorious and majestic are Your deeds. Yes, I am great, glorious and majestic because I am *Your* creation. You are Holy and awesome, Lord. Eternal praise belongs to You. My life is meaningless without You. All creation cries Holy are You, God. We are lifeless without Your Spirit.

Thank You for creating me to praise and worship You in all Your glory . . .

Read:
Jeremiah 17:14; Titus 3:1–2

Dependence on You

I Am Dependent on You, Lord Almighty

Hallelujah to the Lamb of God! You have increased my life! Thank You, God, for the things that You have healed and fixed and mended. I have depended on You to heal me. When I ask, You answer appropriately. My brokenness has brought me to new and exciting places with You, Jesus. You heal my wounds, fix my problems and mend my heart over and over again. I depend on You for these treatments. When I allow You to improve me, You are able to develop others through me. This enrichment advances Your Kingdom. I am obedient and ready to do what is good. Through being dependent on You, I will be peaceable and considerate. Because You have saved me, I will be gentle toward Your created people. The goal is change and spiritual growth in You, Jesus. I am privileged to be part of such a movement of the Holy Spirit.

Thank You for increasing me as I depend on You, Father . . .

Read:
Jeremiah 9:24

Kindness, Justice and Righteousness

O God, You Are the One Who Exercises Kindness, Justice and Righteousness on Earth

You take great delight in these things. I am only a mere frame of dust with Your Spirit living in me. I can only possess these qualities because You are Lord of my life. I depend solely on You throughout the day so that I might put into practice kindness, justice and righteousness. These behaviors are simply impossible for human flesh to obtain. It is by Your Holy Spirit that, not only these, but all things are attainable.

Thank You for letting me share in these beautiful, distinctive attributes with You, my Lord and my God . . .

Read:
Psalm 61:3–4; Proverbs 18:10; 2 Corinthians 12:9–10

Strength

Jesus, You Are My Strong Tower

I take refuge in the shelter of Your wings. I sing praise to Your name. Day after day I seek You. You hear my cry and listen to my prayer. You are my Rock. I am small, and I have many weaknesses, but Your grace is sufficient for me. Your power is made perfect in my weakness. Yes, I will delight in my weakness so that Your power may rest on me. You have made me strong in my weak instances because You are strong. I depend on Your strength to help me through situations of pressure and helplessness. Power and strength belong to me because You are in me. Thank You for Your Spirit that dwells in me.

Thank You for being my strength in my moments of weakness . . .

Read:
Psalm 119:105; Proverbs 2:1–6

Your Word, Your Wisdom

Lord, I Love You, and I Love Your Word

Father, I accept Your words, and I store up Your commands within me. I turn my ear toward Your wisdom. I apply my heart to understanding Your Word. I call out to You for insight, and I cry aloud for understanding. You help me discern the fear of the Lord, and I find the knowledge of God. You alone give wisdom, Lord. From Your mouth come knowledge and understanding. Thank You for the privilege I have in coming to You for these things. Your Word is a lamp to my feet and a light for my path. Thank You, Father, that I am a victor because You desire that Your wisdom be a part of who I am in Christ Jesus.

This is what it means to live . . .

Read:
2 Chronicles 7:14; Nehemiah 9:17

Forgiveness

You Are the God of Forgiveness

How I value Your complete forgiveness, Lord. You are faithful to forgive me. You hear me when I confess my sin to You, Father. My simple act of repentance, by opening my mouth and confessing to You what I have done wrong, brings a world of health to my soul. May I never tire of putting myself in this humble position so that I may be restored by Your healing grace. I will always seek Your face and turn from my wicked ways. I will pray, and You will forgive. You are gracious and compassionate, slow to anger and abounding in love. Thank You for the hidden treasures that are found in repentance and forgiveness.

Thank You for this gift of deep inner healing . . .

Read:
Ruth 2:1–12

Relationship

Praise Be to You, My Lord, Who is the Creator of All People

You have created us to be in a relationship with You and with each other. Your design for us is extraordinary. What a privilege it is to be a part of Your family. Your intentions for me are pure and well planned. I am grateful that You have shown me that I have a purpose in my earthly family and in my heavenly family. You have richly rewarded me in the relationships I have developed with people. I have taken refuge under Your wings, and You have raised me up to blessings. Family is designed and fulfilled through You, Father. May we honor Your arrangements for us. Thank You for creating us to be relational.

Thank You for the comfort of my relationship with You and with others . . .

Read:
Romans 13:8–11; 1 John 4:7–8

Love

You Have Created Everything for the Sake of Love

There would be no point to anything had it not been for love. This is proven through Your Word and through Jesus Christ. Love comes from You, God, and it is Your purpose for everyone in this life to know what love is. Your Word says, "Let no debt remain outstanding, except the continuing debt to love one another, for he who loves his fellowman has fulfilled the law." My life has a purpose, and the fulfillment of that purpose is for me to love. Love is the fulfillment of the law. Everything I do will be right in Your eyes as long as I am doing it out of love, through Jesus Christ. There is no other way. There is no striving to be good enough. Love is the perfect remedy to everything that is wrong in this world. May all of creation wake from their slumber because our salvation is nearer now than when we first believed. Thank You for loving us and teaching us how to love one another.

Thank You, Jesus, for this eye-opening truth . . .

Read:
1 Chronicles 16:25, 31–33, 36

Worship

From Everlasting to Everlasting Your Name Will Be Praised and Worshiped, Father of the Universe

You are great and most worthy of praise, Lord of heaven and earth. You hold the earth in place, and the heavens rejoice. Let the earth be glad. Let the sea resound and the fields be jubilant. The trees of the forest will sing for joy before the Lord. How much more should I! I rejoice in You today, Father! I will declare Your praises wherever I may go. You will give me strength and courage to proclaim Your Holy name in the streets of the place I live. Thank You for choosing me to be Your worshiper.

I will be the one who says God has been good to me. He is my Savior . . .

Read:
James 4:3–10

Submission

O Jesus, How I Thank You for Grace and Humility

You are a faithful and good God with excellent intentions. I understand that this world is temporary and only offers temporary pleasures. I am thankful to You for giving me the grace to comprehend that truth. It is Your deepest desire for me to become like You, Father. I am to submit myself to You, Lord. I am to resist the devil so that he will flee from me. That is extremely powerful! Thank You for opposing the proud, and giving grace to the humble. Thank You for teaching me that my power and strength come by my submission to You, Jesus.

Thank You for instructing me to be humble and submissive before You, precious Savior . . .

Read:
Galatians 2:20

Alive

Christ, You Are Alive and Living Inside of Me

The One who created the entire universe is living in me! Praise the Lord! This is the ultimate gift. My body is inhabited by the Ancient of Days! Glory hallelujah! My God is good to me. The thought of the One true living God taking up residence in my frame runs deep into my soul. It affects the core of who I am. Each day brings a new and utmost degree of pleasure. I am met with joy and delight as You give me satisfaction and contentment. Yes, Father, my gratifications come completely and solely from You. Thank You for giving to me in my areas of need. Thank You for not withholding Your good gifts. Thank You for Your indwelling Holy Spirit.

Thank You for coming to life inside of me . . .

Read:
Psalm 90:12, 14; Proverbs 2:3–6, 10, 20–21

Wisdom

Praise You, Father

You have chosen me! Since I belong to You, I receive Your wisdom daily. I even receive it moment by moment. You have taught me to number my days that I may gain a heart of wisdom. You satisfy me in the morning with Your unfailing love so that I may sing for joy and be glad. I call out for insight and cry aloud for understanding. I know that You give wisdom, and from Your mouth come knowledge and understanding. Wisdom has entered my heart because I have searched for it as for hidden treasure. I walk in the ways of good men and keep the paths of the righteous. I live in the land and will remain in it. Thank You, Lord, for bestowing Your wisdom on me. Thank You for helping me understand the fear of the Lord. Thank You for helping me find Your knowledge. It is pleasant to my soul.

Thank You for choosing to provide me with Your wisdom . . .

Read:
Psalm 9:1–10

Your Name

Your Name is Wonderful

I know Your name, Lord, and I trust in Your name. You have never forsaken me when I have sought You. You are my refuge when I am oppressed. You are my stronghold in times of trouble. You uphold me, and You are righteous. You are just, and You will judge the world in righteousness. Your throne has been established for judgment. You govern the people with justice because You are a good God. I will praise Your name with all my heart. I will tell of Your wonders. I will be glad and rejoice in Your name. I will sing praise to Your name! Thank You, Father, for being trustworthy and faithful to me, Your chosen one.

Thank You for giving me Your name . . .

Read:
Exodus 15:1–18

Strength

You Are My Strength and Defense

I will sing to You, Lord, as Moses did. You are highly exalted. You are my salvation. You are my God, and I will praise You. Lord, You are a warrior. Your right hand is majestic in power, and it shatters my enemies. Who is like You – majestic in holiness, awesome in glory working wonders. In Your unfailing love, You will lead the people You redeem. In Your strength, You will guide them to Your holy dwelling. Lord, You reign for ever and ever. Thank You, God Most High, for Your vigor and justification.

Thank You for the display of Your strength . . .

Read:
Philippians 4:19; 1 Peter 5:10

Sovereign

Lord, You Are Supreme

You know all things. You have planned all things. From the beginning of time, Your plan has been in place. I know that I am safe because You are my Father, and I trust You. Just as a small child has complete trust in their earthly parent, my reliance is in You. When things are going wrong, when I am scared, or when I see potential danger, I have perfect confidence that nothing happens without Your knowledge and allowance. Knowing that You are in control helps me to be able to rest easy, live freely and walk surefootedly. Thank You for Your Word that provides hope and assurance so that I can live without being brought down by the troubles of this world. Thank You for giving me all of Your riches in glory.

Lord, Your sovereignty brings me to a place of rest, peace and freedom. Thank You . . .

Read:
Matthew 7:11; 2 Corinthians 1:20; 1 Timothy 6:19; Hebrews 13:5

Giving

Father, You Are the Giver of All Good Gifts

You give freely and abundantly. Everything You give is for my own advantage. Your desire for me is that I take hold of the life that is truly life. It is not found by anything in this world, but only by receiving and knowing You. I do not want to spend my days searching for something that is not there or chasing after a dream that will never come true. All Your promises are Yes and Amen in Christ. I am going after the One who's promises are true and good. I am choosing to run after the Creator of heaven and earth. I am chasing after the One who loves me without condition and who will never leave me or forsake me. Only You, God, can give these good gifts to Your children of faith. Thank You for giving so freely.

Thank You for giving so abundantly . . .

Read:
Hosea 14

Repentance

Lord, God of All, Your Ways Are the Only Right Direction for Me

I have sin and pain in my past. My sin has been my downfall. With Your loving arms You have bent down to pick me up. Your words have caused me to return to You, my Lord. You forgive all my sins and receive me graciously, that I may offer the fruit of my lips. Nothing in this world can save me. However, in You, the fatherless find compassion. You heal my waywardness and love me freely. You are like the fresh morning dew to me, and I will blossom like a lily. Your splendor is like an olive tree, and Your fragrance like a cedar of Lebanon. I dwell in Your shade. You forgive me when I repent, and You care for me. My fruitfulness comes from You, O God. You give me wisdom and discernment. I understand that Your ways are right, and I desire to walk in Your ways. Thank You for helping me repent so that You may bring blessing. Thank You for opening my eyes to my own shortcomings, Father.

Thank You for forgiving me, Jesus . . .

Read:
Proverbs 4:20–27

Wisdom

God, You Are My Father, and I Am Your Child

As an earthly father gives instruction to his children, so my wisdom and understanding come from You. I pay attention to the details of what You say, and I listen closely to Your words. I will not let Your words out of my sight. I keep Your words within my heart. There they are mine. They are life to me and health to my whole body. I will guard my heart because it is the wellspring of life. I will look straight ahead and fix my gaze directly before me. The paths for my feet are level, and I choose to go in ways that are firm. Thank You for keeping me from swerving to the right or left, Father. Thank You for keeping my feet from evil. You are the most awesome Father!

My life is complete in You, Jesus . . .

Read:
Exodus 26; Ephesians 2:10

Holy Spirit

Praise the Father, Son, and Holy Spirit

I am Your Holy Temple, Lord. You dwell inside of this casing because You chose to. You have constructed me in the same detailed and artistic way that You instructed Moses to build the original tabernacle. You always have the right plans, and Your workmanship is good. Thank You for Your Holy Spirit that resides inside of this temple. I am thankful to house such majesty. What an honor and privilege it is for me to provide Your living accommodations on earth. May I do it with integrity all the days of my life. Thank You, Lord. Your design for things is always perfect.

Thank You for the presence of the Holy Spirit . . .

Read:
Psalm 11:4–5

Assurance

You Are Everywhere Around Me, God, Surrounding Me with Your Spirit

How You can be in all places at all times is a glorious mystery to me. However, I find comfort in knowing that You are omniscient and omnipresent. I have assurance that You are always listening to my prayers, always watching over me, and You always have power over any stronghold in my life. You give attention to my every need. Your eyes examine my righteous soul, and You are perpetually observing my ways. You see things that I cannot, and You reveal productive activity when I choose to believe in Your plans for me. Thank You for opening my eyes so that I may see clearly into heavenly wisdom. Your secluded mysteries are infinitely at my fingertips.

All I must do is seek You, Father God,
and sweet assurance is mine . . .

Read:
John 13:1–17

Example

You Are the Ultimate Example, Jesus

You are my Teacher and Lord. I am Your own, and You have shown me the full extent of Your love. You have washed my feet and given me a place with You in eternity. Your wisdom, imparted to me by the Holy Spirit, has helped me to understand this incredible act of affection. I am to carry this example out into the dying world. By knowing these things from Your Word, I am to set an example to others. You have done a mighty thing, Jesus! Your Spirit is with me as I take what I have learned from You and give it to the broken. I am blessed to do this.

Thank You for being the highest example of blessing and love . . .

Read:
Psalm 119:104; James 1:5

Understanding

Praise You, Jesus, for the Understanding You Have Imparted to Your People

You give generously to all without finding fault. You are full of wisdom. I gain understanding from Your principles. Understanding is something I yearn for, Jesus. I forget sometimes where my understanding comes from. If I will but remember to ask for wisdom, You will faithfully provide for my needs. I will not rely on my own understanding but will trust in You to give me the direction and truth I need to succeed. You are always with me, and You are available for making known to me the understanding I am lacking. May I breathe in Your Spirit, listen for You, and breathe out Your wisdom. Thank You for slowing me down so that I can remember that wisdom and understanding come from You, Father.

Thank You for offering Your wisdom when I but ask . . .

Read:
Romans 11:17–24

Purpose

I Praise You With All My Heart, Father, For Giving Me Purpose

Glory and majesty are Yours, Jesus. You sit on the throne of grace. My soul honors Your existence. It is by You, that all things have come into being. When You spoke, the earth was formed, the waters were placed, and every living creature began to exist. You hold all the power to make everything happen. You even created me to be a part of Your whole plan. I have a purpose. You have grafted me in to Your Kingdom. I am able to stand by faith because You have chosen me to do so. My belief in You gives me nourishment which leads to kindness. You have provided for me in every way, and it is Your desire that I continue to walk with You throughout my days. Thank You for allowing me to be a part of Your world and Your plan. Thank You for supporting me. I praise You with all my heart.

Thank You for giving me purpose . . .

Read:
Jeremiah 29:11–13; Proverbs 3:1–2

Promises and Prosperity

Thank You, Lord, for Fulfilling Your Gracious Promises and Prosperity to Me

You know the plans You have for my life. You want me to be prosperous. You do not want any harm to come to me. You give me hope and a future. I call upon You. I come and pray to You, and You listen to me. You are always available for me. I seek You, and I find You when I seek You with all my heart. Because I keep Your commands in my heart, my life will be prolonged for many years, and You will bring me prosperity. You are faithful to me, God. Thank You for keeping me on the path where Your promises are fulfilled.

Your promises and prosperity are amazing . . .

Read:
Psalm 8; John 15:15

Your Love for Me

Your Love For Me is Amazing

Lord, Your name is majestic in all the earth! You have set Your glory above the heavens. Who am I that You are mindful of me? When I consider the work of Your hands that is before me, I marvel at how You can be thinking of me the way You do. I wonder how You can love me the way You do, yet You crown me with glory and honor, and call me Your friend. You have allowed me to rule over the works of Your hands. Everything has been put under my feet by You. O Lord, how majestic is Your name in all the earth! Thank You for creating the earth, and thank You for being my friend .

I thank You that Your love for me is everlasting and encouraging . . .

Read:
Isaiah 40:31; Mark 12:30–31

Love

My Command is to Love You Lord, My God, With All My Heart, Soul, Mind and Strength

I am striving to love You each day, Lord. Out of my heart flows love that You have placed in it. My soul is utterly committed to You, Jesus. My mind, will, and emotions are committed to You, Lord, because I have chosen to follow You all of my days. My mind strives to stay focused on You throughout the day. My strength, which comes from You, is being renewed because my hope is in You.

Thank You for allowing me to love You with all my heart, soul, mind and strength . . .

Read:
John 14:19; 2 Peter 1:4

Superior

Lord, You Are The Supreme Ruler

You have the utmost power and authority. You see all things that happen in the land. I am a mere mortal, easily discouraged and sometimes fearful. Since I do not know what the future holds, I tend to be afraid of what may happen so, I turn to You, sovereign God, and I offer You my prayers. I tell You about things that frighten and dishearten me. You are always alert and ready to listen to everything I have to say. I tell You my fears and shortcomings, and You encourage and counsel me. I am refreshed when I am in Your presence. I think of Your power, and I know that nothing happens without Your approval. This gives me hope to face uncertain days ahead. Thank You for what You accomplished on the cross so that I may live and stand on Your promises.

Thank You for being evidently superior . . .

Read:
Psalm 149:4; Ecclesiastes 3:14;
John 15:15; Ephesians 1:6; Hebrews 10:22

Relationship

Lord, God, You Are The Ultimate Friend I Want to be in a Relationship With

You endure forever. You are always listening to me, Father. Anytime I need to talk to You, all I must do is choose to begin to utter words, and Your ears are open for me to pour in to You. You are delighted with me, and You take pleasure in me drawing near to You with a sincere heart. Even though You already know all the details and outcome of each day in every situation I face, Your desire is that we communicate beforehand. This communion creates an indescribable sense of serenity in my spirit, and I am more relaxed and calm throughout the day. When the intensity of everyday living begins to arise, I have complete confidence that my God is in control of all things. Your love brings the assurance I need to enjoy peace and happiness each day. Thank You for freely giving me Your glorious grace in the One You love. Thank You for meeting my needs. Thank You for being my friend.

Thank You for our relationship . . .

Read:
Daniel 9:4–19

Daniel's Prayer

You Are a Great and Awesome Father

You keep Your covenant of love with all who love You and obey Your commands. I have known Your Word and have rebelled and turned away. We all have, Father, but I am covered with shame. Forgive me, Father. You hear my prayers and petitions, and You give an open ear to me. You open Your eyes to the requests of Your people, Your righteous, chosen ones, and You have great mercy on us, Lord. You forgive me! You hear and act! You love me, God. This kind of love is supernatural. In the midst of my confession and sorrow, You lift me to higher ground. You tilt my chin up toward Your face and kiss me with righteousness and love. Thank You for answering me in my despair.

Thank You for loving me like Your child . . .

Read:
Isaiah 61:10; Matthew 6:25–34

Provision

Lord, You Are My Provider

You are always looking out for me. You have given to me in all areas, so I lack nothing in this life. Your provision is faithful. You are dependable, God. I know that I am valuable to You, Father. I am a treasure for You to behold. You know what all my needs are. I will not worry about what I will eat or drink or wear. I know You have my tomorrow in Your hands. I am more precious to You than the birds of the air and the lilies of the field. You have clothed me with garments of salvation. You array me in a robe of Your righteousness. I delight greatly in You, Lord. My soul rejoices in You, my God. Your Kingdom and Your righteousness are the things I seek first. Thank You for placing value in me.

Thank You for Your willingness to be my provider . . .

Read:
Psalm 28:8; Psalm 51:11-12

Your Presence

Holy Spirit, Your Presence is a Blessing to Me

I am fully honored to be in Your midst. I worship You while I take this time to be close to You. No other thing can bring me this much joy and peace at the same time. I am anointed by You as I sit in Your presence. I continue to praise and worship You in this holy time of intimacy we share together. Thank You for Your presence, Father. Thank You for Your Spirit.

Thank You for touching me with Your love . . .

Read:
Isaiah 61:10; Revelation 22:17

Salvation

I Delight Greatly in My Salvation, Lord

My soul rejoices in You, my God. As a bridegroom adorns his head like a priest and as a bride adorns herself with her jewels, You have clothed me with garments of salvation and arrayed me in a robe of Your righteousness. Your Spirit beckons me to come. You are relief for my thirsty heart. I wish to take hold of the free gift of the water of life. Thank You for enabling me with the offering of salvation. I am eternally grateful that I have taken hold of this substance You have laid before me.

Hallelujah to the Lamb of God . . .

Read:
Psalm 17:1–8

Prayer

You Are Faithful to Hear My Prayers and Listen to My Pleas, Lord

You are always willing to give ear to my callings, whether in the day or night. You cause my steps to hold to Your path. You keep my feet from slipping. I call on You for all my needs, God. You hear my prayer and answer me. You show me the wonder of Your great love. Your right hand saves all who stretch their hand to You. You have kept me as the apple of Your eye, and You hide me in the shadow of Your wings. Thank You for Your authentic loyalty and steadfastness.

Thank You for listening to my prayers . . .

Read:
1 Chronicles 16:27; Psalm 4:7;
Psalm 16:9,11; John 15:11

Joy

Splendor and Majesty Are Before You, Lord

I gain strength and joy in Your dwelling place. You have filled my heart with great joy. Your joy lies in me, and my joy is complete. My heart gladdens, and my tongue rejoices. You fill me with joy in Your presence with eternal pleasures at Your right hand. I am comforted to know that in any given moment I can come to Your fountain of joy and be filled. Thank You for sharing Your joy with me. Thank You for filling my emptiness with happiness and joy. Thank You for making this joyful path of life known to me.

Thank You for the ultimate benefits I have in knowing You, Father . . .

Read:
Psalm 54:6-7; Romans 12:1; Hebrews 13:15

Sacrifice

My Lips Openly Profess Your Holy Name, Lord Jesus Christ

As I sit in Your presence in this quiet moment, I bring a sacrifice of praise to You, my Father. It is good to be in Your presence, Lord Jesus. You make everything good for me. You help me to understand that I am not alone. You surround me with Your love, and You comfort me. I am free to worship and adore You. I can ask You for help. You give me love and blessings to help me through each day. You deliver me from my troubles, and You help me to see my life in a new perspective - Your perspective. You give me hope, and I have heaven to look forward to. Thank You for giving me freedom to sacrifice myself to You.

Thank You for surrounding me with Your goodness . . .

Read:
Job 1:21; 1 Corinthians 4:20

Praise Your Holy Name

I Praise Your Holy Name Today, Father God

It is not about a perfectly said prayer. There is no formula to getting answers to my prayer requests. It is about giving glory to You, God, my creator, every moment of my life. In good times and bad times, all I need to do is just praise You. As long as my will is in line with Yours, nothing can hold back Your power. I choose not to start my prayers with selfish requests. I choose to begin each day with worship to You, my King. That is what You seek, and that is what is due to You. You created me and then showed me through Your Word what perfect love is. If I am going to ask You for anything it should be for You to show me how to love as perfectly as You do. Thank You for teaching me, Jesus.

Thank You, Father, for allowing me to praise Your holy name each day . . .

Read:
Psalm 16:11; Proverbs 2:6; Philippians 4:13

Relationship

I Am Yours and You Are Mine

In Your presence is where I gain my strength. You make known to me the path of life. I trust You to teach me and to fill me with joy each time we are together. It is through the study of Your Word and listening for Your voice that I gain a heart of wisdom and understanding. You alone can teach me these things in the quiet moments we share together. You are an amazing teacher of truth and goodness. I glean Your teachings, and I am able to approach each situation as You would, Jesus. Eternal pleasures are at Your right hand and You long to share them with me. Through encountering You, I am able to align with You and Your thoughts. You are in me, and I am in You.

I am thankful to You for our extraordinary relationship . . .

Read:
Matthew 6:9–13

The Lord's Prayer

You Are Endless, O God of This Universe

You are immaculate. Your love is never ending. Lord, let Your Kingdom be established in me. Bring heaven down to earth. Show Your beauty to me in a powerful way, so that I may be awed by just a glimpse of Your love. You have captured me with Your splendor, and grace belongs to me. My heart yearns for You. Your power surpasses anything human minds could think or imagine. I cannot grasp Your majesty. Your wisdom is greater than everything. Touch me with only a drop of Your wisdom. Let Your Kingdom be seen by all. Let Your will be done here on earth as it is in heaven. Feed me Your bread daily as I sit in Your presence. Forgive my sins and wipe me clean as I forgive others. Deliver me from all worldly bondage. Yours is the Kingdom and power and glory forever.

Amen . . .

Read:
1 Timothy 6:17

Dependence on You

Praise You, Father, Son and Holy Spirit

Nothing in this world is as certain as Your Spirit. I could chase after anything with value and still end up empty-handed, but with You God, You are the ultimate fulfillment of everything I need. I will not put my hope in wealth or material things. That will all pass away. I will put my trust in You, and I will let my desire be for You alone. You richly provide me with everything for my enjoyment. You are all I need. Thank You for Your provision.

I am thankful to be dependent on You, Lord . . .

Read:
Deuteronomy 7:6; Joshua 1:9;
John 8:12; John 16:33; Romans 8:11

Spirit

Lord of All the Earth, Your Spirit is With Me

You are living inside of me. Your Spirit is alive and active. This truth amazes me. The Holy Spirit of The One and only God of the universe lives inside of my body. I cannot keep from singing praises to You and telling others how magnificent You are. I will not be burdened by the darkness in this troubled world when the light of the world is with me wherever I go. I choose to walk with my head lifted high, a smile on my face and a song in my heart because You have overcome this world. I am saved from the forces of evil. I have chosen to make You my God and King. You have chosen me out of this world to be Your treasured possession. I will be victorious in everything I do today. My GOD lives inside of me. Nothing is more powerful. Your Spirit is a holy gift to me. Thank You for allowing Your Spirit to reside in my soul. Thank You for this gift that thrills and amazes me.

Thank You for giving me the light of life . . .

Read:
Matthew 6:10; 1 Corinthians 2:16;
Hebrews 12:28

Your Kingdom

Your Kingdom Cannot Be Shaken, God

I am thankful to receive Your Kingdom now, here on earth. You deserve acceptable worship with reverence and awe. My praises to You come supernaturally. I acknowledge that You are my Maker. I long to see heaven come to earth each day. You give me eyes to see the hurting and afflicted that surround me. You provide in me, by the Spirit, the ability to do the great things Jesus did. When I give You honor and set my focus on You, Lord, You will show me new and exciting things. When my mind is like the mind of Christ, I cannot be shaken. I receive You, heavenly Father. Your Kingdom is astonishing!

Thank You for this glorious and powerful abundant life in Christ . . .

Read:
Psalm 10:14

Salvation

Praise The Lord, Who Changed My Life Through Salvation

I will not forget the mighty things You have done for me. Every good thing comes from You, God. I am the one You love. You have given me an eternal inheritance by adopting me into Your family. I once was an orphan. You came and saved me. I am no longer fatherless because You helped me find my way. You saw my trouble and grief. You took me in Your arms. I have committed myself to You. You have broken the chains that bound me. You have called me into Your light. You have changed my heart. You have made me complete in You. I will always remember the great things You have done.

Thank You, Father . . .

Read:
Romans 8:28

Who You Are

Lord, You Are Matchless and Infinite

You have given me the ability to know You and Your ways. Your ways are perfect. You have shown me through life circumstances that You are real. You have shown me that You love me. You have shown me that You are with me, and You care about what is going on in my life. You have also given me the ability to recognize how You have worked everything out in my life for my own good. It is Your desire to make sure that I am taken care of, loved, and that I have an understanding of what Your plan is for my life. Thank You for giving me this tender care as only You can.

Thank You for being who You are . . .

Read:
Psalm 146:7–8; Galatians 5:1

Freedom

Freedom Comes From You, Lord

I send praises of love and thanks up to heaven today for being set free by You, Father of my life. Before I knew You, I was subject to a yoke of slavery, but for freedom You have set me free. I will not be burdened by a yoke of slavery ever again. Praise You, Lord. You care for me, and You care for all who need You. You uphold the cause of the oppressed, and You give food to the hungry, but most importantly You set prisoners free. You give sight to the blind, and You lift up those who are bowed down. Submitted to You is where I want to be.

Thank You for providing a position of humility that I can run to and find freedom and dependence on You . . .

Read:
Matthew 19:26; 1 Corinthians 2:9

Dependence on God

Jesus, You Are Closer Than I Can Fathom

You are more real than my mind can conceive. I tend to drift away from Your presence in little spurts throughout the day. I even get caught up in thinking I am doing things on my own. That usually leads to pride and self-righteousness. However, when I stop and think about the One who makes all things possible, You are right there to gently guide my focus back to You and Your glory and majesty. I then praise You and worship You for all You are doing in my life. Thank You for being so real and close to me. Thank You for showing Your love for me through these delicate acts of kindness and care.

You really do love me, God. Thank You . . .

Read:
Leviticus 11:44–45; Deuteronomy 4:24

Set Apart

You Are The Lord, My God, and You Set Me Apart

You are holy, God. You have consecrated me. You are the One who makes me clean and holy. You brought me into this world to be Your own. I am set apart for Your purposes. Your desire is to be my God. You are the Lord my God, and You are a consuming fire. You are jealous for me. You desire my time, attention, and affection. Therefore, I will be holy because You, Lord, are holy. Thank You for dedicating me to Yourself. You have revealed to me how sacred I am to You. Thank You for Your devotion to me.

Thank You for setting me apart . . .

Read:
Proverbs 3:9

Time

I Give My Time to You, Dear Father

My time is precious to You, Lord. You deserve my first fruits in all that I have. It seems that time is the most abundant thing You have given to me, yet it is the one thing I complain about never having enough of. I place myself at Your feet and let the world (and all of its troubles) melt away. As I am in Your presence, You will multiply my time for today. I do not know how You do it, but I know love it. I am grateful for this blessing of time and for this time of blessing.

Thank You, Lord, for helping me remember to give my time to You first . . .

Read:
Romans 3:22–24; Romans 5:1–2

Justified

You Are a Just and Righteous King, O Lord

I lift my hands to You, my Advocate. You have made me righteous through the blood of Jesus. Praise You, Lord! My faith is in You, and I fully believe. I am absolutely aware that I have sinned, and I am entirely justified, freely by Your grace through the redemption that came through Christ Jesus. Yes, I have gained access by faith into this grace in which I stand. I will boast in the hope of the glory of God. I have peace with You, Father. Thank You for Jesus. Thank You for justifying me. Thank You for Your righteousness.

I thank You that I am able to lift my hands in praise to such a righteous and just King . . .

Read:
Isaiah 28:29; John 14:26

Counselor

Lord, You Are Wonderful in Counsel and Magnificent in Wisdom

There is nowhere else I can go for such impelling intelligence. As I come to You with my thoughts and prayers, You lay out a powerful course of action. I am taken by Your will and Your way. I submit myself to You completely so that Your plans may come to fruition. I count on You, the Lover of my soul, to make great things happen through Your effective design. Your direction is impeccably accurate for all. You are my absolute counselor in this life of uncertainty. I run to You with an open heart, and You pour in Your wisdom and love. Thank You for being a certain means of help in a world of confusion and chaos. Thank You for counseling me, Jesus. Thank You for gently reminding me of the things Your Word tells me.

Thank You for teaching me all the things I need to know . . .

Read:
John 15:15; 1 Corinthians 1:9

My All

I Want to Give You My All Today, Lord Almighty

You are righteous and holy. I lift up my voice to give honor to You, my Holy King. Your love is trustworthy and unchanging. I have the confidence I need to get me through each day. You are with me, and You love me. You are my faithful friend. I confide all I have seen, all I have done, and all I am in You. You are closer to my heart than I even know. All my activities and outcomes are in Your hands. I put my trust in Your written promises. You know me so intimately. Not one of my feelings or emotions goes unnoticed by You, heavenly Father. Thank You for creating this bond of love between us. Thank You for teaching me to be dependent on You. Thank You for being a steady resource and friend. Thank You for being my Savior. Thank You for being my comfort and shelter. You are so many different things to me, Lord.

Thank You for being my all in all . . .

Read:
Psalm 37, Isaiah 41:10

Delight

I Am Delighting Myself in You, Lord, Knowing You Will Give Me the Desires of My Heart

I have committed my way to You so that I am dwelling in the land in the safety of Your arms. You make my righteousness shine like the dawn. I am still before You, and I wait for You patiently. I am enjoying great peace in Your presence. You bless me generously because You delight in me. I may stumble, but I will not fall. You make my steps firm, and You uphold me with Your righteous right hand. You strengthen me and help me because You are my God. You are my stronghold. You are The One who delivers me. I take refuge in You and wait for You. Thank You for being so readily available for me at all times.

I delight myself in You . . .

Read:
Matthew 28:19–20; Luke 24:32; John 20:8

Believe

I Believe in You, Jesus

The empty grave proves that You are alive and have risen from the dead. You have conquered death. You have given me hope. I see that You have risen, and I believe. I will go into all the world and preach the good news to all creation. My heart burns within me that all may know the truth. Through the power of the Holy Spirit, You have opened my mind so that I can understand the scriptures. Thank You for giving me the promise of eternal life with You by conquering death. I know all I need to do is believe. Thank You for being alive in me.

Thank You for helping me believe . . .

Read:
Proverbs 22:1; Jeremiah 31:3; Hebrews 4:12

Complete

Only You Can Make My Life Complete

Jesus, I have been on Your mind since the beginning of time. You continue to move in my life because You are always thinking about me and what is best for me. I am overcome with joy and peace just knowing that You are mindful of me. Sometimes I do not think very much of myself, but You have told me differently through Your Word of truth. You tell me that I am better than silver or gold, and that You love me with an everlasting love. Nothing can take that from me, and I am hiding Your words in my heart forever. Thank You for speaking truth into my life through Your Word that is sharper than any double-edged sword.

Thank You for making me complete . . .

Read:
Job 23:10; Isaiah 43:2; 1 Peter 1:7

Faith

My Faith is in You, Jesus

Everything in Your Word is true from start to finish. All praise is to You, my Savior! I have faith in You, Jesus. Being a committed follower has challenged me to look for how You are working in each troubling situation I face. Sometimes I feel like people are downright against me, and there are times when misery and despair seem to overtake my mind. In all this, You are still on Your throne in my heart. I know that You are always working for my good. That means sometimes I may have to walk through a fire, but, I have a clear understanding that I will not be burned by the flames because You are my Redeemer, yet after the testing I will come forth as gold. I understand that You give, and I know that You take away. May Your name be praised forever! Thank You for refining my faith by fire.

Thank You for taking care of all things . . .

Read:
Malachi 1:11; 1 Corinthians 14:2

Exaltation

I Exalt Thee

You are my Lord, and I exalt Thee. You are Christ the Lord. You are the most excellent Father of all the earth. You are worthy to be praised and worshiped. How beautiful are the prayers that overflow from my mouth. You have placed them all upon my tongue. Your Holy Spirit living in me utters words I cannot express. I am a vessel unto You, Father. Your name is great among the nations, from where the sun rises to where it sets. Thank You for Your glory that fills the earth. Thank You for allowing me to exalt You, King of this world.

I exalt You, Father . . .

Read:
2 Samuel 22:17, 19, 33, 37

Revelations

Glory to You, God

You have saved me! When I was wondering around in darkness, Your Spirit spoke to my soul. You reached down from on high and took hold of me. You drew me out of deep waters. You became my support. You opened my closed eyes and made things appear to me that I had never seen before. New, rich colors of clean righteousness were overflowing before me like streams of living water. Only You could reveal such splendor to Your chosen ones. You have broadened the path beneath me, and set me on a new secure way. You are showing me new and exciting revelations. I am seeing clearly now. All glory be to You, my God and my Savior, forever and ever.

Thank You for giving me great revelations . . .

Read:
Psalm 18:30; Matthew 5:48; Romans 8:26–27

Perfection

You Are Perfect in All Your Ways, Lord

You know the beginning and the end of all things. There is no need for me to question Your arrangements. You have set everything in its place. However, You do desire that I commune with You each day. You beckon me to Your bosom so that we may embrace one another in holy fellowship. You even desire that I cry out to You when my words are scarce. Your Holy Spirit is interceding for me with groans that my words cannot express. You search my heart. You know the mind of the Spirit. According to Your will, Your Spirit helps me in my weakness. This is Your flawless plan.

Thank You for clarity and purity through this excellent promise . . .

Read:
Hebrews 12:1–2

Gratitude

Praise You, Lord, For Another Glorious Day Created By You

Thank You for putting enough gratitude in my heart this morning so that I can give You thanks. Thank You for helping me to take the emphasis off of myself so that I can see You first, then others. I admit to being an easily distracted person. It is easy in this day and age that we live in to be intrigued by worldly enticements, but You, Father.... You are the most important priority in my life. Let me throw off everything that hinders me and the sin that so easily entangles. I will run the race marked out for me with perseverance. I am fixing my eyes on You, Jesus, the author and perfecter of my faith. Thank You, Jesus, for keeping me focused.

Thank You for giving me a heart of appreciation and gratitude . . .

Read:
Mark 8:34–38; John 10:10; Romans 5:17

Abundant Life

You Are My Great Teacher and Leader, Jesus

You are The Way to Salvation and abundant life. I praise the works of Your hands. I choose to come after You by denying myself. I will take up my cross and follow You. I will lose my life daily for the sake of the gospel. What good would it be for me to gain the whole world yet lose my soul! I have nothing to give in exchange for my soul. I am in Your hands, Father God. I will not be ashamed of You. Thank You for opening my eyes to Your great and powerful Word, Jesus. You have revealed many things to me, and I will proclaim Your name in this land. Thank You for going before me and preparing the way. Thank You for leading me through. Thank You for giving me opportunities to allow Your Holy Spirit to bring others to salvation.

This is abundant life . . .

Read:
Psalm 48:10; Acts 1:8; Colossians 2:13

Holy Spirit

I Have a Master in Heaven

Lord, You extend to a great height! My heart is thrilled to worship Your holiness. You are exceedingly dignified and elevated in majesty. Your power, authority and praise reaches to the ends of the heavens and earth. I have received Your power through the Holy Spirit that has come upon me. I am Your witness. You protect me and guide me. I am able to do astounding acts of love and kindness in Your Name through the power of the Holy Spirit living inside of me. These things do not come naturally to me because I am made of flesh – the dust of the earth. With You, however, I can do the miraculous. You have made me alive with Christ. Thank You for infusing Your Holy Spirit into my entire being. Thank You for giving me power and authority through the Holy Spirit. All aspects of my life are in Your hands, Father.

Thank You for Your Holy Spirit . . .

Read:
Psalm 40:2–3; Mark 11:10

Praise

Lord, You Are The One I Will Praise All of My Days

There is no other that can compare to You, Jesus. Even when I do not feel like praising You, I will do it. I will not relent. It is in the times when I do not feel like praising You that I will do it the most. Those are the times that I will shout glory to Your holy name. I will sing of Your excellent greatness. I will cry out Hosanna in the highest, and praise be to God the Father for His unfailing love. Today is the day I will say I love You, Jesus. Thank You for accepting my praise. It is in these times that You will lift me up and set my feet on a solid rock. You will liberate my soul, and You will cause Your greatness to fall fresh on me. Praise be to You, heavenly Father!

I praise Your wonderful name . . .

Read:
Psalm 100

Worship

I Shout For Joy to You, Lord

I worship You with gladness. I come before You with joyful songs. I know that You are God. You made me, and I belong to You. I am Yours. I am the sheep of Your pasture. I will enter Your gates with thanksgiving. I will enter Your courts with praise. You are good, Lord, and Your love endures forever. Your faithfulness continues through all generations. I give thanks to You, Father, this day and forever and ever. Thank You, Jesus!

I am so blessed that I can worship You . . .

Read:
Deuteronomy 26:18;
Ezekiel 37:4–5; 1 Timothy 6:19

Life

Just to Know You, Father, Brings Life to My Dry Bones

Just to be loved by You is better than all I can imagine. I am Your treasured possession, and You are mine. We have this relationship that is built on mutual trust and adoration. No other relationship is quite like ours. My time spent resting in Your arms is better than life. Your love for me is unending. I strive to be with You throughout the day and build on our relationship as much as I can. I am trying to think about You all day long. I even want my dreams to be consumed by You when I am sleeping. I want to know You more and more. Thank You for allowing me the honor to know You.

Thank You for letting me take hold of life that is truly life . . .

Read:
Galatians 5:22; Colossians 1:11;
Colossians 3:12

Patience

You Are a Kind and Patient God

You are slow to anger. You abound in love. The amount of patience You have for me is incredible. I am amazed at how You never try to rush me. You simply wait quietly for me to make my decisions. You do not even have an adverse reaction to me if I make the wrong choice. When I fail and fall, I come to You. You pick me up, hold me close, give me a clean slate and set me on my way. I am restored in Your presence. Your peace washes over me. I have all these things because You are a patient God giving grace to Your child. I, myself, am striving to posses Your kind of patience. I want simplicity and forbearance to be abundant in me. My efforts are not going unnoticed by You, Father. When You and I are in agreement mighty things happen, and blessings begin to flow in bombastic quantities. Thank You for modeling patience for me. It gives me an honest depiction of what patience truly looks like.

Thank You for Your unrestrained patience with me . . .

Read:
Psalm 112

Blessing

You Are My Personal Blessing, Lord

I find great delight in Your commands, Master. You have blessed my generation. You have blessed me with wealth and riches that cannot be seen. You have been able to cause me to be righteous through Your Son, Jesus. You have also caused me to be gracious and compassionate. Goodwill has come to me because You have opened my eyes and taught me how to be generous and lend freely. You have equipped me to conduct my affairs with justice. I will not be shaken. I do not live in fear. I am blessed. My heart is steadfast, trusting in You, Lord. My heart is secure, and I look to the end with triumph. You alone have made me righteous and blessed, O God.

Thank You for being my blessing . . .

Read:
Joshua 24:15

Service

You Are What I Choose to Put My Trust in All the Days of My Life, Dear Father

Serving You is a choice, Holy Lord. This day I will choose for myself to serve You, Lord. I have counted the cost. I have recalled Your deliverance for me. I have pondered Your protection. I have delighted in Your provision. I have resolved to follow You. It is a confident choice You have put in my mind, and my heart overflows with joy as I serve You. Thank You for gentle, sweet reminders of the ways You have touched my life through Your unfailing grace given to me. I can do nothing less than serve You, my Faithful Friend.

How amazing our journey is together . . .

Read:
Isaiah 28:6; Matthew 11:28; John 14:27; 1 John 3:1

Provider

Jesus, You Are My Soul Provider

Your supplies are never-ending. I receive peace, love, strength and power from You. My spirit senses when I am running low or feeling weak by the way I react to my surroundings. I know where my source for all provisions comes from, and You are always ready and faithful to fill me back up to overflowing with Your endless supply of resources. I do not have to strive in this life. I do not have to empty the bank. I do not have to use my own strength. Your Spirit is here for me to draw from. May I rest in the truth of what Your Word tells me. I will come to You for restoration. Thank You for providing rest, love, strength and power.

Thank You for being my unending source . . .

Read:
Genesis 1:26–27, 2:7;
1 Corinthians 6:17–20

Honor

I Honor You, Jesus, With My Entire Self

I am united with You, Father. You are The Creator of this temple, and Your Holy Spirit resides within my soul. I am created in Your own image, in Your likeness. I am a living being because of Your purpose to bring me in to action in Your world. I am walking in supernatural strength and living out what You have planned for me to do. I represent You in all my actions and when others look at me, I want them to see You. Thank You for showing me that I am not my own. I have been bought at a price. I will honor You with my body and with my actions.

Thank You for honoring me by uniting us together in one Spirit . . .

Read:
Micah 6:8; Nahum 1:3, 5 & 7

Good Favor

You Are Great in Power and Most Worthy of All of My Praises, Lord God

You are good, Lord. You are my refuge in times of trouble. You show good favor to those who trust in You. The mountains quake before You, and the hills melt away. The earth trembles at Your presence. The clouds are the dust of Your feet. Immeasurable power exists within You, Father of all the living. You are the creator of power and authority. I am in awe that my supreme Maker would care so deeply for the details of my life that You would be my shelter and safe place. What an awesome God You are! You have shown me what is good, Lord. I will act justly. I will love mercy, and I will gladly and boldly walk humbly with You. Thank You for this significant advantage of being loved and favored by You.

Thank You for showing me good favor . . .

Read:
Psalm 70

Rescue

Glory to You, God

Lord, You are the great rescuer. You have come to my rescue, Lord. You came quickly to help me and to save me. I will rejoice and be glad in You. In my times of need You always come through for me. I discover You in new ways with each trial I face. Your plan for me is good, even when it seems things are not going according to the way I think they should. When things look dark You are faithful to bring Your light. I trust that You are in control. My freedom comes from You, Jesus. By Your Spirit, I was willing to allow You to come into my heart and save me. I said, "I believe in You, God." By these actions and words, You brought me into Your eternal Kingdom.

Thank You, Father, for rescuing me quickly and saving my soul. I give You glory . . .

Read:
Proverbs 3:7–18; James 1:5

Wisdom

You, Lord, Are The Holder and Giver of All Wisdom

I am not wise in my own eyes. My wisdom comes from You, Lord. You grant wisdom to me when I ask for it. I am blessed when I receive Your wisdom. Through You I can gain understanding. Your wisdom is more profitable than silver and yields better returns than gold. It is more precious than rubies. Nothing I desire can compare with Your wisdom. My ways will be pleasant and peaceful when I seek Your wisdom. It will be a tree of life to me when I embrace it.

Thank You, Father, for the impartation of wisdom to my soul . . .

Read:
Exodus 33:22; Job 29:4; Galatians 4:6–7

Intimacy

I Am Close to You, Lord, and I Feel Your Presence Surrounding Me in This Very Place

You have given me the freedom to be with You wherever I am. I can do that with no one else. I am Your child, and You have made me an heir. We are going through this life together, hand in hand. You are never going to leave my side. You put me in a cleft in the rock, and You cover me with Your hand. I invite You into the depths of my soul. You see my innermost thoughts and feelings, and there is an indescribable measure of intimacy between You and I that will live forever. What an advantage I have in knowing You. Thank You for choosing me, Abba. Thank You for staying close to me.

Thank You for hiding my soul in the depths of Your love . . .

Read:
Luke 18:1; Hebrews 12:2–3

Persistence

Father, You Are Far More Than Good to Me

You are the giver of all things. You give each of us abilities according to Your purposes. You have given me the ability to be persistent. Persistence, when properly exercised, brings about abundant blessings. Many a true character has been developed through the act of persistence. I consider that You endured much opposition, yet You did not give up. You have been my inspiration so that I will not grow weary or lose heart. You are the driving force within me that is increasing my character. If it were anything other than You, Father, all would be false and in vain. Thank You for helping me to keep my eyes fixed on You, Lord. I will always pray and not give up.

Thank You for teaching me value of being persistent . . .

Read:
Psalm 118:22; 1 Peter 2:4–7

Cornerstone

Jesus, You Are The Key to Life

You are the most excellent! You are the capstone! You are the finishing touch to everything. What You have done is marvelous in my eyes. I hold You in the highest regard. You stand firm in all my dealings. I cling to You, the One the builders are unwilling to accept. You are the living Stone – rejected by men but chosen by God and precious to Him. You are my precious cornerstone, and I trust in Your strength to uphold me. I believe in You, Father. Thank You for giving my life support with Your valuable finishing touches.

I cherish the work of Your hands that is done within me . . .

Read:
Psalm 27:13–14; Psalm 92:5

Your Presence

I Bless and Honor You Today, Lord Jesus

I have come this day to love, adore, and worship You, holy King of Kings. I enjoy being escorted by You during these times in the quiet of the day. This is the time when important matters come to my mind, and You are able to speak wisdom into each situation for me as I walk with You and listen attentively. You are faithfully assisting me as I wait patiently. I breathe in Your love for me as I come to a motionless quiet place. How deep Your love is for me. You bring things to my mind that I cannot see on my own. You work wonders in ways that I cannot conceive. You are powerful, and You are profound in all of Your thoughts. I see Your goodness in the land of the living. Thank You for being consistently involved in all of my dealings. Thank You for being so faithful every time I come to You.

Thank You for the excitement of a new day
with new blessings in Your presence . . .

Read:
Psalm 150:1, 6; Galatians 5:22–23

Praise

May Everything That Has Breath Praise You, Lord

I praise You in Your mighty heavens. I praise You in my feeble heart. Your acts of power are worthy to be praised. You have mercy on me, You heal me, and You love me. You have performed countless miracles. You deserve more than honor. You are the greatest! Your ability to relate to me leaves me speechless. I am in awe of Your great love for me. What compassion, patience and understanding You have for Your children. You are kind, faithful, and gentle. Thank You for teaching me love, joy, peace, patience, kindness, goodness, faithfulness, gentleness and self-control.

I belong to You, and I will keep in step with
Your Spirit by praising Your Holy name . . .

Read:
Galatians 5:13–18

Spirit

I Praise Your Spirit, My Father

You are leading me with Your Spirit. I am living by Your Spirit. If I am led by the Spirit, I am not under the law. I do not want to gratify the desires of the flesh. Those desires are contrary to the Spirit. Rather, my desire is to be led by the Spirit so that I may walk in freedom. You have called me to be free. I am to love my neighbor as myself. I can fulfill the entire law by keeping this one command. How powerful! Thank You, Father, for giving me freedom. Thank You for choosing me to be Your child. Thank You for helping me to be obedient.

Thank You for leading me with Your Spirit . . .

Read:
Psalm 68:19; Matthew 11:28–30; John 15:13

More than a Friend

You Are More than a Friend to Me, Lord Jesus

I do not bear my burdens alone, God. You are right here with me. It is beneficial for me to carry everything to You in prayer. I know that You are aware of everything that is going on with me. You are what a true friend looks like. I am pleased to be able to talk to You about things that I simply cannot handle on my own. You are my carrier of troubles. I am blessed by Your willingness to make my load lighter. You honor me by allowing me to bring things to You and ask You for help through perilous times. Thank You for this freedom of being able to just lay everything at Your feet anytime I need to. Thank You for bearing my yoke with me.

Thank You for being more than a friend . . .

Read:
Hebrews 12:7–12

Discipline

I Praise You For Discipline, Lord

You have made a way for me. My life has not always been easy. I have had many hard times. However, You, Father, have been faithful to help me to see things through Your eyes. I have endured hardship as discipline. I am aware that You treat me as a child. For what child is not disciplined by their parent? We who belong to You will certainly undergo discipline because we are true children. Your discipline is always for my good, that I may share in Your holiness. Although it is painful sometimes, later on it will produce a harvest of righteousness and peace. I am being trained by You, God. You are strengthening my feeble arms and weak knees. You are helping me make level paths for my feet so that I am not disabled, but rather healed! Praise You, Lord!

Thank You for discipline, Jesus . . .

Read:
John 1:29; 1 Peter 1:18–19; Revelation 5:12

Worthy is the Lamb

Praise Be to You, Jesus, the Precious Lamb of God, Without Blemish

You are the ultimate and perfect sacrifice that takes away the sins of the entire world for every generation. Glory to Your name, Father of all nations. You rise among all others, and Your wisdom exceeds any who have ever been and all who are to come. Blessed be Your name. Worthy is the Lamb who was slain, to receive power and wealth and wisdom and strength and honor and glory and praise. I am redeemed from the empty way of life by Your precious blood.

Thank You, Jesus . . .

Read:
Exodus 14:14; Deuteronomy 1:29–33

Fight

Glory to You, Lord

The victory is won! I trust in You, Father! You are the One who fights for me. You will go ahead of me on my journey. I will not be terrified or afraid. You have already gone before me, and You are my Fighter. You fight for me before my very eyes. I have seen how You have carried me, as a father carries his son. You help me reach all the destinations You have searched out for me. You show me the way I should go. I only need to be still. You are the One who takes up my spiritual conflict. I will allow You to do my fighting for me. You are so much better at it than I am. Help me to take the time that I would normally spend trying to fight my own battles, and turn it into a time of prayer in the secret place with You. Thank you for allowing me to depend on You to win my battles. Thank You for combating the enemy for me.

Thank You for allowing me to acknowledge that You have already won the victory . . .

Read:
John 3:16; 1 Corinthians 13:4–8;
2 Corinthians 5:14; Ephesians 2:4–5

Love

Your Love Overwhelms Me, Father

You give Your love so freely and with such purpose. You are genuine in all Your expressions of love to me. You poured out Your love to me by the giving up of Your Son to save me from eternal damnation. Your love is patient, kind and true. You protect me with Your love, and I am able to stand and walk in confidence and victory. Your love never fails. Thank You for compelling me to live for You by showing me just how much You love me through Jesus Christ.

Thank You for expressing Your great love for me . . .

Read:
Exodus 34:8, 29; Psalm 18:35–36

Worship

Praise, Honor, Worship and Adoration belong to You, My Holy Lord

You are my Counselor and King, my Redeemer and Friend. You are Emmanuel and Jehovah God. I bow as my heart ponders Your many names. I take all I am and surrender to Your perfect will. I hear more clearly when my posture is yielded to You in submission. I am humble at Your feet. I bring myself down to be affected deeply and completely. I subdue myself at the feet of my Savior. I worship You, and You address me gently. As we express our desires to one another, we are uniquely uplifted. I am radiant after our encounter and eager to meet the day. My time spent with You is precious, Lord. Thank You for stooping down to make me great. Thank You for loving me where I am. Thank You for broadening the path beneath me.

Thank You for teaching me what true worship really looks like . . .

Read:
Psalm 121; Hebrews 4:16, 13:6

Confidence

I Have Complete Confidence in You, O Lord

You allow me to approach Your throne of grace with confidence so that I may receive mercy and grace to help me in my time of need. You are my helper. I will not be afraid. No one can do anything to me. I belong to You, and You protect me. In my times of fear I will run to You. I lift up my eyes. My help comes from the Lord, the Maker of heaven and earth! You are always watching over me Lord, as a father watches over his child to ensure their safety and well being. You keep me from harm as You watch over my life. I thank You for looking after my coming and going both now and forevermore. This is what gives me the great confidence I have in You, dear Father.

Thank You . . .

Read:
Matthew 7:13–14

Journey

How Good it is to Be Coming Together With You, Father

I bless Your Holy Name. You freely shower Your blessings on me. You do not withhold goodness from my presence. Your message of grace for me brings peace to my mind and comfort to my soul. I am able to walk in righteousness because of You, my Lord. It is a direction I am delighted to be traveling. You walk with me and talk with me along this journey. You keep me on the straight and narrow path that leads to everlasting life with You, my Creator. Thank You for being with me every step of the way. I am learning who You are more and more with each meeting we have together. This is a privilege to me.

I am blessed by Your presence on my journey through life . . .

Read:
2 Corinthians 4:16–17

New Beginning

You Are The God of New Beginnings

You make all things new. Inwardly, I am being renewed day by day. I do not lose heart. These light and momentary troubles are achieving for me an eternal glory that far outweighs them all. I am refreshed by You, Lord. I sit in Your presence, and I am automatically changed. Your transforming power alters me as I study Your Word and talk with You about it. I welcome this modification of character gladly. Only You could make this happen. It raises me up to new heights. Thank You for affecting me in this way. Thank You for making all the difference.

I praise You, Lord, for letting me start over and have a new beginning . . .

Read:
Psalm 21:6

Fulfillment

We Complement One Another Well, Dear Jesus

I am full. Each day is a new adventure with You, Lord. My worship goes to You in every way today and always for such a fun-filled, activated life in Your presence. My happiness and joy come from You, Jesus. The junk that the enemy tries to throw my way in a day, will never stand up or last. I am pressing into the One who fights my battles for me. I find complete wholeness in You, Father. Nothing can fill me up the way that You do. You have granted me an unending supply of blessings, and You have made me glad with the joy of Your presence.

Thank You for creating the fulfillment of delight and pleasure in my inner soul through Your Holy Spirit . . .

Read:
Isaiah 55:9; John 10:10

Ultimate Plan

Thank You For Planning My Life, Jesus

You have the ultimate plan. It is perfect. It is for me. My goal is to submit to it. Your ways are higher than my ways. Your thoughts are higher than my thoughts. Therefore, Your plan is going to be greater than any plan I could ever think of or imagine. My way is not the best way. Thank You for opening my eyes to that. When I have chosen to submit, and Your ultimate plan is in place, I am able to enjoy ultimate blessings, ultimate freedom, and ultimate intimacy with You. I am not willing to settle for a cheap imitation of what my life should look like. You came so that I can have life and have it to the full. I surrender to Your plan of excellence – the best way. I thank You for helping me to leave things to Your discretion. Thank You for teaching me to yield.

Thank You for Your plan of perfection . . .

Read:
Isaiah 52:13; 53:3–5, 10–12

Pouring Out

You Have Poured Out Your Love For Me, Jesus

You are lifted up and highly exalted! My sins were many, but You, Father, acted wisely. Although You were despised and rejected, You took up my infirmities and carried my sorrows. You were pierced for my transgressions. You were crushed for my iniquities. The punishment that brought me peace was upon You. And by Your wounds I am healed. Thank You, Jesus, for bearing my many sins. Thank You for making intercession for me, the transgressor. Because You poured out Your life into death, I am now able to live. This was God's will for my life from the beginning. I praise the One who gave me life.

I praise You for pouring Your love out and into me . . .

Read:
Matthew 8:23–27

Calming the Storms

Jesus, You Calm All My Storms, and I am so Thankful For You

You have already climbed in the boat ahead of me, before the waters begin to move. Without warning, furious storms may come upon me. I say, in the name of Jesus, I am *not* going to drown! My faith is strong, and I am not afraid. I am not alone. You arise and rebuke the winds and the waves. You make everything completely calm. I stand amazed in Your presence. Even the winds and the waves obey You. Thank You for never leaving my side. Thank You for staying in the boat with me.

Thank You, Jesus, for calming all the storms in my life . . .

Read:
2 Corinthians 5:14–15

Love

Thank You For Being Loving Toward Me, Lord

Thank You for loving me for who You made me to be. I thank You, God, that Your love for me is not based on my performance. There is nothing I can do to make You love me anymore than You already do. Nothing I can do will make You love me any less. Your love for me is without conditions. You require nothing from me. My belief and praise are simply what I long to do each day as You love me. Your goodness to me compels me to worship You, Father. My heart is what leads me into worshipping You daily. Nothing else could cause this kind of obedience and dedication. This is supernatural. Your love is better than life so Your praise will ever be on my lips. You are all I want, Lord. Thank You for this dynamic relationship You have developed between us.

Thank You for loving me . . .

Read:
Isaiah 40:6–9

Everlasting Word

Your Word Stands Forever, God

The grass withers and the flowers fall because You blow Your breath on them, but Your Word stands forever! I am like grass, Lord, but You are a holy God that raises me up to righteousness through Jesus Christ. Praise You Lord! I lift up my voice with a shout of praise to You, Father, and I am not afraid. You are my Savior, and I am proud to be called a child of the King. Thank You, Lord for the privilege to worship You freely. Thank You for giving Your powerful Word to me.

Thank You for giving me Your everlasting Word that will stand firm forever . . .

Read:
Isaiah 6:3; Amos 4:13 & 5:14

Lord Almighty

You Tread the High Places of the Earth, Lord God Almighty

You have formed the mountains, and You have created the winds. The whole earth is full of Your glory. I will seek You. I will seek good and not evil that I may live. Lord You are with me just as You say You are. I feel Your presence through the Holy Spirit. I close my eyes and see visions of You in heaven above seated on Your throne of grace. You are a majestic image for my eyes to behold. I am in awe of Your splendor. Thank You for giving me a picture of hope through Your Word.

Thank You, Lord Almighty, for holding this world in Your prodigious hands of love . . .

Read:
Psalm 27:14; Proverbs 19:11

Patience

You Are The God of Perfect Timing

You have everything planned from beginning to end. You have all things in Your hands. I am completely satisfied knowing that You are in control and that I belong to Your Kingdom. Being content on a regular basis, however, can seem out of reach sometimes. Even though I struggle with patience and waiting, I know that You are teaching me to be more like You, Jesus. I will wait for You, Lord. I will be strong and take heart, and I will wait for the One in whom I have placed my trust. Thank You for teaching me to let everything be accomplished in Your perfect timing. Thank You for holding the whole world in Your loving hands.

Thank You for granting me patience . . .

Read:
Isaiah 61:7–62:1

Salvation

I See Your Righteousness, God, and I Worship You

You have shown me salvation. It is like a blazing torch. You have doubled my portion this day as I sit in Your presence. Everlasting joy is mine! You are known throughout the earth, and Your faithfulness is seen in every land. Your righteousness springs up before all nations. You love justice, Lord. You exercise Your mercy on me daily. I acknowledge that I am one of Your chosen people, and I am blessed. You have created a pure and clean heart in me because of Your loving heart toward me. It was not anything I did, but because You chose me. I am overwhelmed with adoration and worship for my Father today.

Thank You for causing me to be filled with fine distinctions of truth so that I can carry out the salvation and righteousness that You have infiltrated into my very being . . .

Read:
Psalm 150

Praise

Let Everything and Everyone Praise You, Lord

You deserve the highest honor. You are the great King. Your glory surpasses all others. Your love for me is deeper than any other. You have proven Your presence to me time and time again. I see Your mighty hand at work. You spoke the world into existence. The grass, mountains and rivers are Yours. You hold the universe in Your hands. You have created Your sons and daughters for Your glory. May everything that exists give You the highest praise. You make all things hold together. We are the brothers and sisters of Christ, and we will sing Your praises.

Thank You for being our King . . .

Read:
Isaiah 53:6–11

All for Love

Your Love For Me is Endless, Elohim

I, like a sheep, have gone astray. I have turned my own way. You have laid my iniquity on Yourself. You were oppressed and afflicted, yet You did not open Your mouth. You were led like a lamb to the slaughter, and as a sheep before her shearers is silent, so You did not open Your mouth. By oppression and judgment, You were taken away. You were cut off from the land of the living and sent to a grave though You had done no violence. No deceit was in Your mouth, yet Your will was to be crushed and to suffer. After the suffering of Your soul, You saw the light of life and were satisfied.

Thank You for this rich abundant love only You can give . . .

Read:
Ephesians 2:8; 1 Timothy 1:14

Grace

Your Grace is Amazing, Lord

I have received it effortlessly. What a most beautiful gift! This act of compassion toward me brings me to my knees in reverence to You, Lord of Lords. How You must love me, yet I have nothing of any value to offer You. You require nothing of me but my heart. That is what You are interested in, God. Your eyes are upon my inner being. You are constantly looking at me with loving open arms. This is what is so amazing about Your grace. It is why this gift is set apart from all other gifts. It is unmerited favor.

Thank You for the outpouring of love You have shown to me through Your grace . . .

Read:
Isaiah 40:10–11

Shepherd

O Sovereign Lord, You Come With Power, and Your Arm Rules For You

You tend Your flock like a shepherd. You gather Your lambs in Your arms, and You carry them close to Your heart. You gently lead those that have young. You do these things because You love me. Thank You for such strength You reveal through Your pure motives. Thank You for carrying me and leading me gently by Your Spirit. This quality of life is incomprehensible. Thank You for making a way for me to live in the comfort of Your arms through Jesus Christ.

Thank You for being my Shepherd . . .

Read:
Psalm 20

Support

I Trust in Your Holy Name, Lord

You are my built-in support. You save Your anointed ones. You answer from Your holy heaven with the saving power of Your right hand. You give me the desires of my heart, and You make all my plans succeed. You give me help and support, and You accept me. You protect me, and I am victorious. I have sought You, and I cannot be shaken. I rise and stand firm. I will lift up my banner in the name of my God and King. Thank You, Father, for saving me. Thank You for accepting my praises to You.

Thank You for being my ultimate support . . .

Read:
Psalm 25:10

Attributes

All Your Ways Are Loving and Faithful, My Beloved Savior

You are clothed with grace and mercy. It is Your innermost desire that I experience these attributes. You have given me favorable circumstances to receive certain measures of love, faith, grace and mercy. We stay closely connected through these characteristics whether You are lavishing them on me or teaching me how to show them to others. I thank You for the ways You freely rain down these choice qualities and share them with me. Everyday life circumstances are constantly available for You and I both to exercise these attributes in me. May I accept every opportunity.

Thank You, Jesus, for giving me love, faith, grace and mercy . . .

Read:
Zechariah 9:9–10; James 5:11

Gentle

You Are a Gentle King, O God

Your rule extends from sea to sea, Lord of heaven and earth. You proclaim peace to the nations. You are great, almighty and powerful, yet You came to us righteous and having salvation, gentle and riding on a donkey. You hold all wisdom and authority in Your hands, and You distribute it among Your people according to Your personal provision. All the while having great compassion and mercy for Your entire creation. There is none like You, Holy God. Thank You for showing me Your true heart through the life of Jesus. Thank You for teaching me humility and grace through Your Word. Thank You for granting me salvation. I honor You, Father.

Thank You for being gentle with me . . .

Read:
Jeremiah 32:27; Mark 4:41; Mark 9:23

Possible

I Am Beholding Your Beauty and Grace Today, Father

Nothing is impossible with You, God. Nothing is too hard for You. You are the Lord, the God of all flesh. Everything submits to You, Father of the entire universe. Even the wind and the waves obey You. You are incredible to all who encounter You. When the world and my mind are telling me, "It can't be done" or "It will never change," You remind me that the victory is already won. I recall Your scriptures that tell me everything is possible for one who believes. My eyes and focus are gently turned back to Your promises. Keep me in this place with You, Lord. Thank You for making a way for me to put my hope and trust in what is good and true. Thank You for going before me and preparing the way. Thank You for giving me the ability to submit to Your perfect plan.

Thank You for making all things possible . . .

Read:
2 Timothy 1:8–12; Hebrews 4:15

Life

You Have Called Me to a Holy Life, God, Because of Your Own Purpose and Grace

Even though I may have to experience a little suffering throughout my days, I am thankful I am in a relationship with the One who suffered all things and can sympathize with my weaknesses. You have been tempted in every way just as I am. Nothing I can do will make my life any more holy. It is only through Your grace given to me in Jesus Christ. I will continue to suffer for the gospel as Jesus did because death has been destroyed. Life and immortality have been brought into light through the gospel, yet I am not ashamed. I know who I believe in and I am convinced that He is able to guard what I have entrusted to Him for that great and glorious day when I see His face.

Thank You, God, for Jesus . . .

Read:
Psalm 91:4; Isaiah 4:2–6

Protection

Lord, You Are a Great Shelter and Sanctuary For Me

You are my Protector. You are beautiful and glorious. I am a survivor in this land because You have stretched out Your wing to me and covered me with Your feathers. This is where I find refuge. You call me holy even though I do not feel that I am. You have washed away my filth and cleansed my bloodstains by a Spirit of judgment and a Spirit of fire. You shelter me and shade me from the heat of the day. You are my hiding place from the storm and rains. Thank You for protecting me. Thank You for Your provision that drives me forward to survival mode here on this earth. It is good to be in Your sight. It is comforting to have Your Spirit living inside of me.

Thank You for protection, heavenly Father . . .

Read:
Jeremiah 31:13,
1 Thessalonians 1:6, Philemon 7

Your Will

You Refresh My Heart Each Day, Father

I know what Your will is for my life! Praise You, Lord. Your Word tells me I am to be joyful always, pray continually, and give thanks in all circumstances. You give me comfort and joy instead of sorrow, and Your Holy Spirit gives me joy in the midst of severe suffering. Your love has given me great joy and encouragement. I will converse with You in my mind and out loud all the things that I need to talk to You about each day. I will never allow our line of communication to be closed. You desire that I commune with You throughout each day. Whether things are good or bad, I will give You thanks. I cannot control many circumstances, however, You have granted me the fruit of self control, and in having it I will praise Your name in all things. This is Your will for me... to be happy, talk to You all the time, and to say "Thank You." Thank You for giving me joy and thankfulness. Thank You for allowing me to keep an open dialogue with You throughout each day.

Thank You for refreshing my heart and for revealing Your will to me . . .

Read:
2 Corinthians 6:1–2

Salvation

O Jesus, Now is the Time of Your Favor

Today is the day of salvation! You have heard me, and You are helping me! Thank You Jesus! What an honor and privilege it is to come before You with worship in my heart. I open wide my heart to You, Father. I will not withhold one thing. You deserve my utmost and highest praises. I am so devoted to You, and You encourage me. Thank You, Holy One, for accepting my worship to You. Thank You for saving me from this wicked world. Thank You for listening to me. Thank You for helping me. I receive Your grace.

Thank You for granting me salvation . . .

Read:
Acts 20:32; 1 Thessalonians 5:11;
James 3:9–10

Praise & Encouragement

May My Tongue Only Glorify You, Heavenly Father

May these lips only remit praises unto a holy God. My tongue was created to praise You, Lord, yet with it, I have cursed men, who have been made in Your likeness. I know this should not be. Your Word of grace has built me up and given me an inheritance among all who are sanctified. Your Word teaches me to encourage the people You have created and build them up. I am to communicate Your message of love to all whom I encounter. It is only by me making a conscious effort, with help from the Holy Spirit, that I can accomplish this great task. I am built up by You when I choose to obey. Your desire is for all Your children to praise You. I will emit Your presence in me to others. I will do this by glorifying You in all I do – in words, in deeds, in everything. Thank You, Lord, for helping me to see that my words have meaning. Thank You for encouraging me through Your Word and for teaching me to encourage others.

I praise Your Name . . .

Read:
2 Corinthians 1:21–22

Worship

I am Lost in Worship With You, Father

Praises from deep within me have no choice but to escape into Your presence this glorious morning, Lord. It is nothing difficult for me to show You my honor and adoration each day. It is very simple. I only need to take the time to do it. My life is not so busy. Worshiping You is important to me. My day only fills up with activities that I allow. It is You, God, that makes me stand firm in Christ. You have anointed me and set Your seal of ownership on me. You put Your Spirit in my heart as a deposit guaranteeing what is to come. My love for You is rich and intense. It is fitting that I fall deep into worshiping You each day.

Thank You for making my simple act of worship such a special time between us . . .

Read:
Psalm 55:22; Isaiah 40:29; 1 Peter 5:7

Strength

I Am Gaining Strength in You This Day, Lord

You have allowed me to cast my burdens and cares on You. You are the One sustaining me. You will never let the righteous be shaken or fall. I know that You care for me because You have given me strength in days of anxiety and worry. I look to You in difficult circumstances, and You always bring me through the times of peril. Thank You for caring so deeply for me when things are good and when things are bad. I will always remember to praise You on good days and on bad days. You give me strength when I am weary, and You increase power within me when I am weak and at Your mercy. Thank You for such an important promise of hope in hard times.

I honor You with the strength You have provided me in this life . . .

Read:
1 Samuel 2:30; Proverbs 3:9;
1 Corinthians 6:20; Revelation 4:9–11

Honor

All Honor Belongs to You, Lord

I worship and honor You, Jesus. I honor You with my body. I honor You with my wealth. I honor You with my praises. It all belongs to You anyway, Lord. Jesus, You are holy. You sit on the throne, and all the living creatures give glory, honor and thanks to You who lives forever and ever. I will fall down before You and lay my crown before the throne. You are worthy, my Lord and God, to receive glory and honor and power. For You created all things, and by Your will they were created and have their being. Honor is due to You, Jesus. Your Word says You will honor me because I honor You. In all I do, may I honor You.

Thank You for allowing me to honor You . . .

Read:
Romans 15:5–6; 1 Corinthians 6:17

Unity

Hallelujah to The One Who Unifies Me With Himself

I love the way our relationship has developed, Lord, and how we have become unified in our hearts and minds. You have drawn me unto Yourself, dear Father. You are gentle and trustworthy in all Your ways. I am united with You in perfect unity. I am one with You in Spirit. You have also given Your children a spirit of unity among the ones who follow You. May we glorify You, the God and Father of our Lord Jesus Christ, with one heart and mouth.

Thank You for the blessing of unity . . .

Read:
Psalm 91:9–16

Protection

Glory to My Mighty Rescuer and Protector

You, Most High, are my dwelling place. You are my refuge. I call upon You, and because You love me, You rescue me. You are with me in trouble. You do not allow harm to befall me. No disaster comes near my tent. You command Your angels concerning me to guard me in all my ways. They lift me up in their hands so that I might not strike my foot against a stone. You empower me to tread upon the lion and the cobra. I will trample down the great lion and the serpent. You protect me because I have acknowledged Your name in all my ways. You deliver me and honor me. You satisfy me with long life. You have shown me Your salvation. Thank You for being my dwelling place, Lord.

Thank You for protecting me, and thank You for loving me, Father . . .

Read:
Jeremiah 31:35

Highest Praise

You Deserve the Highest Praise, O Lord

You appoint the sun to shine by day, and You decree the moon and stars to shine by night. You stir up the sea so that its waves roar. The Lord Almighty is Your name. Your blessings are endless. Even in all Your majesty You take the time to care so much for me. Your eyes are on me day and night. I give You the best of me. I give You the first and the most. I am overflowing with gladness. My praises are a sweet sound in Your ear. The best I can bring to You, Lord, is my very highest praise. I delight myself in You, Jesus. And You, being the loving and caring Father that You are, give me the very best blessings. You give me the desires of my heart.

Highest praises and thanks go to You, Abba . . .

Read:
Psalm 119:45; John 8:32;
2 Corinthians 3:17; Galatians 5:1, 13

Freedom

You Are The God of Freedom

You have given me much liberty, Jesus. I walk about in freedom. I seek Your direction. Your Spirit is on me, Lord, because You have anointed me to proclaim good news to the poor. You have sent me to proclaim freedom for the prisoners and recovery of sight for the blind. You have sent me to set the oppressed free. You are the Spirit, Lord, and where Your Spirit is there is freedom. It is for freedom that You set me free. I will stand firm, and I will not let myself be burdened again by a yoke of slavery. I was called to be free. I do not use my freedom to indulge the flesh, rather I choose to serve my brothers and sisters humbly in love. As I walk in the freedom You have given me, I am blessed by You, King. I know the truth and the truth has set me free.

Thank You for freedom . . .

Read:
1 Corinthians 14:37; Galatians 5:16;
Philippians 4:13

Spirit

I Know Full Well That Your Spirit is With Me, Abba Father

It is crucial that I walk according to Your Spirit. I want every word I speak to be in alignment with what the Spirit would want me to say. Every action I take will affect my surroundings. Therefore, I will be listening to the Spirit that comes from You, Almighty God. When I love, let it be the love of You, Father, so that others will see You, not me. Your Spirit living in me can reach millions. I can do nothing without You. However, I can do everything through You. You are the one who gives me strength. Your Spirit has given me many gifts, and I am walking in them. Thank You for spiritual gifts. Thank You for teaching me how to walk in them as I sit in Your presence.

Thank You for Your Spirit . . .

Read:
Psalm 118

Thanksgiving

I Give Thanks to You, Lord

Your love endures forever. You are good. I will not die but live! I will proclaim what You have done. Your right hand is lifted high and has done mighty things. I will tell of what Your right hand has done for me. When I have been hard pressed I cried to You, and You have been my helper. You have opened the gates of righteousness for me. I will enter and give thanks to You. You have saved me. You have made Your light shine upon me. You have granted me success. I bless Your name, Jesus. I give thanks to You. You are good, and Your love endures forever. I am giving You thanks today. You are ever deserving.

I am thankful that it is You I can give my thanks to . . .

Read:
Ephesians 2:10

Life

I Thank You For My Life Itself, Father

You created me, God. I worship You. You knew what You were doing when You chose to bring me into Your world. My life is filled with many divine purposes all managed and ready to be fulfilled by You. You have the ultimate authority over every facet in my life. Thank You for choosing me. Thank You for setting me in motion.

Thank You for life . . .

Read:
Romans 8:14–17

Kinship

I Belong to You, Father

I praise You! I am led by Your Spirit, and I am a child of God! I have not received a spirit that makes me a slave again to fear, but I received the Spirit of sonship. I cry Abba, Father, and Your Spirit testifies with my spirit that I am Your child. If I am Your child, then I am an heir. I am an heir of You, God, and I am a co-heir with Christ. I have chosen to share in the sufferings of Christ so that I may also share in His glory! Amen! I am a child with privileges.

Thank You, Jesus, for this eternal promise of kinship . . .

Read:
Isaiah 45:1–6

The Lord My God

You Are The Lord, and There is No Other

You have called me by name, and You take hold of my right hand. You have gone before me through all of my life circumstances. You level the mountains in front of me as they rise up against me. You break down the gates of bronze and cut through bars of iron. You give me the treasures of darkness and the riches stored in secret places so that I may know that You are the Lord. I acknowledge that You are the Lord my God and there is no other. From the rising of the sun to the place of its setting, I know there is none besides You, Lord. You are where my strength and ability come from. You know me, and You love me. You take care of me and, I praise Your Holy Name. Thank You for being the Perfect Lord. I am so grateful. There is none like You, Father.

Thank You for being the Lord, my God . . .

Read:
Psalm 26:3; 1 Corinthians 15:42–44

Supernatural

Lord Jesus, You Are on My Mind Today

I am keeping my thoughts far from this world and close to the Spiritual truth of Your Word. I am not thinking in the natural but in the supernatural. This is where I will be able to see You, feel Your presence, and walk according to Your design for me. This is the meeting place where my expectations of life are exceeded by Spiritual awakenings. This is a place of comfort and encouragement. This is where I turn my worldly thoughts and views into praises and thanksgiving to my supernatural King. Thank You for filling my mind with praises for You, Father.

Thank You for giving me the desire to focus on my Savior and King . . .

Read:
Psalm 27

Salvation

You Are My Light and My Salvation

Whom shall I fear? You are the stronghold of my life. Hallelujah! There is nothing for me to be afraid of. If anyone tries to attack me they will stumble and fall. I will dwell in Your house, Lord. I gaze upon Your beauty, Jesus. I seek You in Your temple. In my days of trouble You keep me safe in Your dwelling, hiding me in the shelter of Your tabernacle and setting me high upon a rock. You hear my voice when I call, O Lord. You are merciful to me and You answer me. You do not hide Your face from me. You do not reject me or forsake me. You receive me, teach me and lead me in a straight path. I will see Your goodness in the land of the living. I am waiting for You, my Lord. I am strong and I take heart; I am waiting for You, Lord.

Thank You for saving me . . .

Read:
Matthew 14:25–33

Your Love for Me

You Have Drawn Me in and Wrapped Me in Your Love

Praise You, God! I will keep my eyes fixed on You today. I know that things will come against me, but You will come to my rescue. I should not be afraid. The maker of the universe is on my side. You tell me to come to You out on the water, just as Peter did. I take courage, and I am not fearful. I bravely step out of the boat. I come toward You with my entire being fixated on the One who loves me. You reach out Your hand to me. If my eyes begin to wander, You lift me back up on the water. I, in turn, worship and adore You. I say, "Truly You are the Son of God."

Thank You for Your love that lifts me up . . .

Read:
Ezekiel 34:26

Blessings

Praise Be to My Heavenly Father Today For Waking Me Up This Morning and Blessing Me

I have so many things to be thankful for. I have so many blessings to count. I will count them throughout the day today and give You all the glory for each one You have placed. I am not discouraged in anything I do because You have given me great motivation to live for You. You have chosen me to share Your glory with this generation. I am overwhelmed with many good things from You, Father. I can breathe easy knowing You are in control of all things, and I am in Your hands today and forever. Thank You for giving me an attitude of praise, worship and thankfulness today!

Thank You for showers of blessings . . .

Read:
Philippians 4:12–13

Contentment

Life Just Keeps Getting Better and Better With You, Lord

You have blessed me through the years and You keep on giving and giving. I have been content with You as my soul provider. I know what it is to be in need, and I know what it is to have plenty. I have learned the secret of being content in any and every situation, whether well fed or hungry, whether living in plenty or in want. I can do everything through You, Lord. Thank You for giving me Your strength. Thank You for taking care of me through every season of my life. Thank You for reminding me that You are my provider in every way. Thank You for meeting all my needs.

My life is content and blessed by You . . .

Read:
Isaiah 66:1–2

Humility

Heaven is Your Throne, Lord Almighty, Who Reigns on High

The earth is Your footstool. You are so awesome, God. I praise You. Your hand has made all things so they came into being. You esteem the one who is humble and contrite in spirit. You hold in high regard those who tremble at Your Word. My soul is Yours, and my life is laid down before You, Father. I humble myself before Your holiness, and You heap blessings on me as I rest at Your feet. Righteousness is mine because Your Spirit lives inside of me. Thank You for being an all-powerful God. Thank You for bringing me into being, and thank You for opening my heart to humility through Jesus.

My life is in Your hands . . .

Read:
Genesis 2:7; Job 12:10; Psalm 16:11;
Psalm 41:12; Isaiah 42:6

Abundant Life

God, Thank You For Breathing Your Breath of Life Into My Nostrils

You have made me into a living being. Before I knew You there was no life in me. I had no fullness of joy. Now, here in Your presence, You have made known to me the path of life. Eternal pleasures are at Your right hand. You are delighted to take good care of Your children. You uphold Your creation and set me in Your presence forever. Your hand holds the life of every creature and the breath of all mankind. Thank You, Creator, for taking hold of my hand and keeping me.

Your Spirit has made me, and Your almighty breath has given me abundant life . . .

Read:
Jeremiah 17:14; Malachi 4:2

Healing

You Are The Great Physician, Lord Jesus

Healing is one of Your most powerful tools in softening my heart. You bring healing to me daily, and I praise You for this gift that comes even without my acknowledgement. You are so very subtle in Your grace and mercy. I look forward to the day when the sun of righteousness will rise with healing in its wings. I will go out and leap like a calf released from the stall. You have given me hope for healing today and eternal healing for the future. Thank You for giving me the faith I need to be healed. Thank You for healing me every day, dear heavenly Father.

How I love Your healing touch . . .

Read:
John 15:16

Chosen

You Are Valuable to Me, Lord

I hold the utmost reverence for You. You chose me, and that is precious to me. I cherish the thought of the King of the entire universe thinking about me when He chose to create a world full of diverse people. I cling to the idea that You love me so much. You have appointed me to go and bear fruit – fruit that will last. You depend on me to ask You for things so that You can bless me with answers. I will always ask in the Name of Jesus. How I value our relationship! My mind is in a state of love when I cleave to these necessary truths for living in this darkened world. Thank You for the assurance of Your beautiful promises.

Thank You for choosing me . . .

Read:
Lamentations 3:58;
Luke 1:68; Galatians 3:13–14

Redeemed

All Praise Be to My Redeemer, Jesus Christ

You have recovered me from a debt that I could never afford. You see me as Your redeemed saint. Lord, You redeemed me from the curse of the law by becoming a curse for me. It is by my faith in You that I have received the promise of Your Holy Spirit. Praise be to You, Lord, because You have come to me, and You have redeemed me. You took up my case and redeemed my life. Thank You for clearing my payment. Thank You for paying the price for me.

Thank You, my Lord, for delivering me and redeeming me . . .

Read:
Isaiah 56:1–8

Chosen by Name

I Love Your Name, Lord God.

I worship You. I worship Your name. Your Name is glorified and lifted high. I will do my best to maintain justice and be righteous. I will choose to do what pleases You, Father. You will give me a place in Your house. In Your walls, You will give *me* a place and a name. You will give *me* an everlasting name. I join myself to You, Lord. I hold fast to Your Word, and I love Your Name. Your name is wonderful, yet You have chosen *me* by name. You will bring me to Your holy mountain and make me joyful in Your house of prayer. You accept me just the way I am. You have gathered me to Yourself, and You love me in Your arms. Thank You for Your glorious name. Thank You for Your everlasting Word. Thank You for taking me on and taking me in.

Thank You for giving me a name that will endure forever . . .

Read:
Isaiah 58:11; 1 Timothy 6:6

Guide

Lord, You Are My Guide in Everything I Do

You satisfy all my needs in this sun-scorched land. You strengthen my frame every morning when I rise. I am like a well-watered garden, like a spring whose waters never fail. You have taught me what it is to be content, and godliness with contentment is great gain. I do not need anything this world has to offer. I find my rest and peace in You, God Almighty. I know You will never leave me. You will never forsake me.

Thank You, Father, for keeping me by Your side and for being my guide . . .

Read:
2 Corinthians 3:7–18

Spirit

Lord, You Are The Spirit, and Where Your Spirit is, There is Freedom

The ministry of Your Spirit within me is glorious. Your glory will last through eternity. The hope of this glory gives me boldness. When I turn to You, You take away the veil and set me free. Yes, You have unveiled my face, and I reflect Your glory. I thank You and praise You, Jesus, for the gift of the Spirit, which comes through Christ Jesus. Thank You for revealing things to me through the new covenant. I am being transformed into Your likeness with ever-increasing glory which comes from You, Lord, the Spirit.

Thank You for Your Holy Spirit . . .

Read:
Psalm 85

Favor

You Show Favor To Me, Lord

You are the ultimate Father. You set aside all Your wrath, turn from Your fierce anger and restore me to the fullest. You have shown me Your unfailing love and granted me salvation. I am listening to what You have to say by reading Your Word diligently. You promise peace to me, Your saint. Love and faithfulness meet together; righteousness and peace kiss each other. Lord, You will indeed give what is good. Righteousness goes before You and prepares the way for Your steps. You are always ready to lavish Your favor and love on me.

I receive it, and I say thank You to my Father . . .

Read:
Psalm 37:37; James 4:10

Worship

My Entire Focus is on You Today, Father

I am sinking into a position of humility at Your feet and authentically praising and worshiping You from my heart. I know when I take my eyes off of myself and my own problems and pity, my vision becomes unclouded as though I am looking through Your eyes, Father. You are the One that deserves all of my focus and strength. I take time today to put my efforts toward You. In doing this I am assured through Your wonderful Word that I will gain strength, understanding, love and peace. You are amazing, Abba! Thank You for keeping Your promises to me.

There is nothing better than worshiping You . . .

Read:
Psalm 67; Psalm 86:15

Graciousness

How I Praise You, My Gracious God

You have been gracious to me. You have blessed me and made Your face shine upon me. You are praised by the people of the nations. You are guiding the nations, and You rule the people justly. May I allow You to use me so that Your ways may be known on earth. May all the people on earth receive salvation through You. It is not Your desire that anyone should perish. You are a gracious God, slow to anger and abounding in love. You are compassionate and faithful to me. Thank You, Jesus. You are with me, and You love me.

Thank You for being gracious to me . . .

Read:
1 John 3:16–18; 1 John 4:7–12

Love

Love Comes Only From You, God

Jesus, You have taught me how to love by laying down Your life for me. I, being in Christ, ought to lay down my life for my brothers. I will love with actions and in truth. When I see another in need, I will have pity on him because the love of God is in me. You have chosen me to love Your people. I am born of You, God, and I know You. Your love is so great for me that it makes me want to love others. I know You live in me, and Your love is made complete in me. I am very thankful to You for showing me these truths.

I praise Your name for the love only
You can pour into my soul . . .

Read:
2 Corinthians 5:20; 1 Peter 2:9

Salvation

Thank You For Another Day to Praise You For My Salvation, Lord

I praise You for giving me an attitude of unbroken belief in You. Your plan for me is simple and good. You have created infinite trust for me to embrace as Your chosen one. May I represent You well. Thank You for opportunities to step out in faith and exercise my salvation. I will accept the challenges of the day and put to practice the truth I learn from reading Your Word. Thank You for ranking me in such high regard to be a living breathing illustration of the One true God.

This important position in my salvation is vital for Your Kingdom, and I praise You for showing me this favor . . .

Read:
2 Timothy 2:18–26

Pure Heart

My Heart Belongs to You, God

I am fully and completely Yours. You know the ones who are Yours. I confess Your Name, O Lord. I call on You out of a pure heart. You have removed from me foolishness and resentment and replaced them with kindness and gentleness. You lead me to the knowledge of truth. I am only taken captive by You, Father God. You know me, and You love me. I speak these words of truth over my life because You have saved my soul. My heart is important to You. You will me to know You and love You. Thank You that my heart matters to You. Thank You for showing me just how much You care for me.

Thank You for giving me a pure heart . . .

Read:
1 John 3:1–20

Your Child

Lord, I Have a Sense of Belonging With You

Your love for me is so great that You call me Your child, and that is what I am. I am not even as magnificent as I am going to be yet. When You appear I am going to be like You! I will see You as You are. My hope is in You, therefore, I am purified, just as You are pure. It is a privilege and an honor to be called a son or daughter of You, God. I do not continue to sin because I am born of You, and Your seed remains in me. I am fully aware that I belong to the truth. I set my heart at rest in Your presence when my heart condemns me. Jesus, You are greater than my heart, and You know everything. Thank You for laying down Your life for me.

Thank You for making me Your own . . .

Read:
Lamentations 3:22–24; Philippians 4:11

Thankfulness

It is With a Grateful Heart That I Lift My Hands in Praise to You Today, Lord of Heaven and Earth

I look around Your world and see Your blessings and Your created beauty. It is in the atmosphere around me. I must open my eyes and heart so that I can see it and acknowledge it. You have new and exciting treasures for me to enjoy each day. I want to wallow in Your unending blessings and grace, not self-pity or unhappiness. You have provided greatly for me. Your mercies are new every morning. Great is Your faithfulness to provide vivid life for me to bask in with Your creations. The Lord is my portion, says my soul, therefore, my hope is in You, Father of all creation. May I turn my mind toward thankfulness and be content with what You have blessed me with.

Thank You for laying gratitude on my heart today . . .

Read:
Luke 13:10–17

Healing

I Praise You, Lord, the God of Healing

I am loosed from every form of bondage this world has tried to restrain me with. Lord, You set me free from my infirmities. You straighten me, and I glorify You, Father God. You teach me when I read Your Word. You call to me, and You immediately make me fully straight. My belief that You can do this is my motivation for returning to Your presence for healing. Thank You for being fully faithful so that I can be fully healed.

Thank You for continually healing me . . .

Read:
1 John 4:13–19

Spirit of Love

You Have Given Me Your Spirit, God

I know that I live in You and You in me. I acknowledge that Jesus is Your son. I know and rely on the love You have for me. I know there is no fear in love. Your Word tells me that perfect love drives out fear. You are perfect, Lord. Fear has to do with punishment. The one who fears is not made perfect in love. I know it is Your desire that I am made perfect in love. The only reason I know how to love is because You loved me first. God, You are love. Thank You for allowing Your Spirit to live in me.

Thank You for Your love . . .

Read:
Matthew 11:28; Philippians 4:4–7

Rest

I Am at Rest in My Heart Knowing You, Lord, Are My Savior

I come to You, Father, and You give me sweet rest. You understand that I have labored and that I am heavy laden at times. You give me peace that passes all understanding. I trust in You with all my heart. I am not anxious about anything because I have given You thanks and prayed, and I have presented my requests to You. You are guarding my heart and my mind. I am rejoicing in You, Lord, always. I am letting my gentleness be evident to all. Lord, You are near. The peace that I feel only comes from You.

Thank You for this quiet time of rest in my heart and life . . .

Read:
Philippians 3:3–11

Confidence

My Confidence is in You, Lord

I worship You by Your Spirit. I put no confidence in the flesh. The confidence I have comes from You. I trust You, Jesus. Nothing compares to the surpassing greatness of knowing You, Jesus. I have gained You, Jesus, and everything else is rubbish. I am righteous only by the cross and my faith. I am happy to be found in You, so we will fellowship together, and I will share in Your sufferings, becoming more and more like You. You are my ultimate goal. Thank You for giving me the confidence I need through Your Word to work toward my dreams of being like You. Thank You for letting Your Spirit rest on me moment by moment.

Thank You for embellishing me with great confidence . . .

Read:
Philippians 2:1–2

Unity

You Are The Creator of Unity, Lord of All

I am encouraged from being unified with You, Christ Jesus! Your love gives me comfort. You have granted me tenderness and compassion because I am united in fellowship with Your Spirit. This has caused me to be in unity with my fellow brothers and sisters in Christ. We are like-minded, having the same love because of You. We are enabled by You, O God, to be one in Spirit and purpose. May the world know that we are Christians by the love that we share with them freely. Thank You for uniting Your people.

Thank You for showing us how to love by uniting Yourself to us through love . . .

Read:
Psalm 68:19, Matthew 11:28–30

Laying Down My Burdens

You Are The Maker of All Things, and You Are Bigger Than All Things

Nothing is too arduous for You to handle, God. Nothing is too trivial for You either. You look at my smallest matters with care and concern. I know that You are handling all things. Whether I am caught in a huge problem or a tiny issue, You are there in it with me. You always see me through it. Your desire is that I lay my burdens at Your feet daily so that I can walk easy and light. What a tremendous act of love You have shown me through this. Thank You for giving me rest for my soul when I am weary. Thank You for managing my difficulties whether they are large or small.

I am thankful I can lay them down . . .

Read:
Romans 13:1–7; 1 Timothy 2:1–4

Called to Pray

You Have Put All Things in Place in Your World, Lord, God of Heaven and Earth

Every governing authority has been established by You, Father. I am called by You to submit myself to the governing authorities and to pray for my leaders. They are Your servants, and You have placed them in their positions. I will honor and respect what You have established in Your creation. In doing so, I am being obedient to Your Word. You also promise that I may live a peaceful and quiet life in all godliness and holiness. This is good and pleasing to You, Lord. Thank You for giving me wisdom about these things. Thank You for being in control.

Thank You for calling me to pray for Your people in Your establishment . . .

Read:
Matthew 4:23–24;
Romans 15:17–19; Hebrews 2:4

Revelations

My Heart Praises You Today, Father

You have revealed Your great and mighty works of healing and restoration in many lives in Your world. I have seen Your miraculous signs and wonders. I have witnessed Your healings and salvations. You have shown me great and wonderful things. I am in awe of Your goodness to Your people. My faith is strengthened by Your mercy and grace given to me and to Your people who cry out to You. You have been an excellent God from the beginning, and You continue to thrill me with the answers You give to my prayers. Thank You for caring for me and accepting me. Thank You for thrilling my heart with a fresh touch from Your Spirit each morning. I am content in being in Your presence. Thank You for showing me who You are.

Thank You for revealing great wonders to me . . .

Read:
Psalm 93; Revelation 4:11

Honor

You Are the One I Honor, Lord Jesus

You are Holy and Praiseworthy! I honor You with my mouth. From my soul I raise up worshipful praises to You. You are robed in majesty and armed with strength. Your world is firmly established by Your mighty hand, and it cannot be moved. I do not set my focus on worldly idols. My praise belongs only to You, Jesus. You have empowered me to be who I am, and I will honor You with my actions and my being. I will carry myself in ways that glorify You and point others toward Your majesty. Your statutes stand firm, and holiness adorns Your house for endless days. Thank You for letting me be a part of Your majesty. Thank You for this calling to praise You in all I do.

Thank You for allowing me to honor You with all I am . . .

Read:
Psalm 37:4; Ephesians 3:20–21

Answered Prayer

You Are My God Who Hears My Heart's Cry

Praise You Jesus! You answer me with a display of blessings that only come through the power of the Holy Spirit. You are teaching me each and every day how to be patient and wait for You to bring about the changes that need to take place. You are always so faithful to do all the work, Lord. All I must do is give You honor and commune with You each day. It is pleasurable for me to submit myself to Your perfect plans. Life is so much more orderly and comfortable when I sit back and allow You to come up with the solutions to my prayers. You are much better at working things out than I am. You are able to do immeasurably more that anything I ask or imagine according to Your power that is at work within me. Glory to You, God! Thank You for giving me the desires of my heart as I delight myself in You.

Thank You for hearing my hearts yearnings and for answering with divine and supernatural outcomes . . .

Read:
Philippians 4:11–13

Sufficient

I Bless and Honor Your Holy Name This Morning, Lord Jesus Christ

You make every day worth living. I am a fulfilled, strengthened living-being when I am walking through my day with Your presence surrounding me. With You, Christ, I am never in need. I have seen difficult days and trying times. I have even been in need, yet I know how to find my way and walk with a humble spirit about me. You have given me plenty, and through You I have learned the secret of being content in every situation. Thank You for empowering me with strength to do all things which You will show me. Thank You for making me self-sufficient through *Your* sufficiency. Thank You for infusing me with confident peace and inner strength.

You are enough . . .

Read:
Genesis 1:27–28; Colossians 1:19–20

Power

There is Power in Your Name, Jesus

There is power in Your blood. All power and authority come from You, Holy One. You created power, You set it up, and You give and take it away from whom ever You choose. You created mankind and You blessed us. You gave us the earth to multiply on it and to subdue it. You give us the authority to have dominion over every living thing in it. I am blessed to be Your creation. Your power brings unspeakable joy. It is beauty for my soul to behold. I am humbled in Your sight and in Your presence. May I bring glory to Your holy name in all I do through the power You have placed in me by the shedding of Your precious blood on the cross. Thank You for granting power to Your people.

Thank You for giving us power and authority to use in Your name . . .

Read:
John 15:14–15; Hebrews 13:5

Friendship

You Are the Perfect Friend, Jesus

I deeply value our relationship. In the quiet times when we meet together, I know intimacy is being formed. When I meet with You regularly I will know You more. I will begin to see how You work in my life and how You speak to my heart. I want my heart to be connected to Your heart constantly. I feel and sense Your presence when there is a connection between us. My connections with people come and go throughout the day as I am in and out of their presence, but You, Holy Spirit never leave me or forsake me. I am standing on that promise as I remain in You and You in me. Our relationship is like no other. We will never end.

Thank You for being connected to me . . .

Read:
Psalm 40

Praise

Lord, You Have Put a New Song in My Mouth

It is praise to You alone. Many will see You, fear You and put their trust in You. How blessed they will be. You have planned many wonders for me. You are incomparable. If I were to speak and tell of Your deeds they would be too many to declare. My mouth is open unto You to proclaim Your praises. You have opened my heart and given me a desire to do Your will. I do not hide Your righteousness in my heart, yet I speak of Your faithfulness and Your saving help. They are my protection. All who seek You rejoice, and they are glad in You. Those who long for Your saving help say, "The Lord is great!" You are my new song, Lord, and I will praise You all day long.

Thank You for opening my mouth to declare praises to You . . .

Read:
2 Chronicles 1:12;
Proverbs 3:1–3, 5–6; James 1:5–6

Wisdom

Thank You for Granting Me Wisdom, Father

I lack wisdom, and I ask You for wisdom. You give generously to me without finding fault. I will not forget Your teachings. I will believe and not doubt. I will keep Your commands in my heart. I know this will prolong my life many years and bring me peace and prosperity. Love and faithfulness will never leave me. I have bound them around my neck and wrote them on the tablet of my heart. I trust You, Lord, with all my heart. I do not lean on my own understanding, but I acknowledge You, dear heavenly Father, in all my ways, and You are making my paths straight. Thank You for softly directing me toward Your wisdom when my heart wants to go its own way. Your love for me shows through Your gentleness. This kind of assistance is impeccable.

Thank You for supernatural wisdom
through Your living Word . . .

Read:
Romans 3:23–24; Colossians 1:13–16

Love

I Praise You for Loving Me, Lord

Our relationship is not based on what I do or say. It is based on Your love for me, Jesus. My performance will not bring me any closer to You, my Maker. I am at my best when I choose to be still and receive Your love. That is when I am filled to overflowing. It is Your grace that tells me how much You love me each day. Nothing I say or do can make You love me any more or any less. You do not change the way You feel about me if I stumble or fall. You are always consistent in our relationship to love me, wait for me, forgive me, cleanse me, and direct me. You created me, therefore, You love me. I am blessed and overjoyed at Your love for me.

Thank You for loving me no matter what . . .

Read:
Romans 8:2; Romans 15:7; Colossians 1:12

Your Presence

You Are Ravishing, Father God

You are the first thing I want to see in the morning when I open my eyes. What a beautiful way to start the day. It is in that rare moment of the day that You can speak to me about the events of the day and how I am to handle them. You already know where You are going to take me and where I am going to need the most help. As I sit quietly and enjoy Your presence, I can glean truth about who You are and who I am in You. I choose to believe the things Your Word tells me, such as, I am beloved, accepted, qualified, established, set free, alive, blessed and victorious! My life is in Your hands each day as I rise. I will go about my day walking in Your Spirit because Your morning presence has filled me to overflowing.

Thank You for letting me rely on this time of fulfillment to set me on my way . . .

Read:
Psalm 145:8–9

Compassion

Lord, You Are the God of Great Compassion

You have this love for Your people that is filled with never-ending sympathy. You are gracious and compassionate, slow to anger and rich in love. You are good to all, and You have compassion on all that You have made. I am encouraged today to have compassion like You, Father. I am grateful for Your compassion to me. May I show those around me just a glimpse of the compassion that You have shown me, Jesus. Your love and empathy penetrate my heart toward moving into action for Your Kingdom. Thank You for showing me compassion so that I may bless others through what You have given to me.

Thank You for being merciful toward my feelings . . .

Read:
Ephesians 5:8–20; 1 Peter 2:9

Light

You Are the Light of the World, Jesus

I declare Your Praises, Lord. I sing and make music in my heart to You, Lord. I will always give thanks to You, Father, for everything, in the name of my Lord Jesus Christ. For I was once darkness, but now I am light in You, Lord. I choose to live as a child of light. Everything exposed by light becomes visible. You have awakened me from sleeping. You have raised me up from the dead, and You are shining on me, Jesus! You give me wisdom so that I will make the most of every opportunity, because the days are evil. I will choose to be filled with Your Spirit! I will build up others and tell of the ways You save and rescue the weak and dying.

Thank You for calling me out of darkness and into Your wonderful light . . .

Read:
John 15:1–9

Remain

You Are the True Vine, Jesus

I am Your branch. I am to bear fruit so that You will be able to prune me and so that I can be ever more fruitful. I am already clean because of the word You have spoken to me. I receive Your Word, and I remain in You, as You remain in me, Lord. I cannot bear fruit by myself. It is imperative that I stay connected to You, Father. Apart from You, I can do nothing. I will show the world that I am Your disciple by bearing much fruit from remaining in You. I know this brings glory to You, Father. You are the only One I want to be connected to. Thank You for allowing me to remain in Your love.

Thank You for loving me . . .

Read:
Matthew 16:16; Luke 9:23–24

Hero

You Are the Ultimate Hero, Lord Jesus

My shouts and cheers are for You, Father! You have won the victory and defeated the enemy and therefore, I have! It is glorious and comforting to know that I am on the winning side. My days ahead are happy and absolute. You are the Messiah, the Son of the living God. I give praise to my Master. You have conquered the grave. Thank You for allowing me to experience triumph as I take up my cross and follow You each day. I am fascinated at Your divine plans. I am overwhelmed and overjoyed as I lift up my Victor in praise and veneration. Thank You for sharing this conquest with me.

Thank You for being my supreme champion . . .

Read:
Psalm 3:8; Psalm 18:2; Psalm 72:12–13

Deliverance

You Are My Deliverer, Jesus

I regard You with great awe and devotion. You are my rock, my fortress and my deliverer. You are the One who has come to my rescue. Deliverance comes only from You, Lord. You have been faithful to deliver me when I am needy and afflicted. I cry out to You, and You hear my voice. You save me, and You take pity on all who are weak, needy and have no one to help them. It is crucial that I remember to cry out to You for deliverance whether my circumstances seem small or large. You are the way to being delivered from anything that tries to bring me down. I look forward to seeing how You will help me.

Thank You for being so trustworthy to deliver me in all my conditions . . .

Read:
1 Chronicles 16:8; Hebrews 12:28

Thanksgiving

I Give Thanks to You, Almighty God

You are the source of my being. All things come from You. You are the fountain from which all blessings flow. Your supply is plentiful and unending. All things that come from You are good and trustworthy. I show my thankfulness and reverence through worshipping You, Jesus. I give thanks to You because You have done great things. I see the works of Your hands. I will make known the things You have done. I will proclaim Your goodness to the people. My heart is glad as I look into the beauty of Your world. I hope for the heavens with what my eyes have already seen.

I am thanking You today, Father. You are good to me . . .

Read:
Psalm 63:3; 1 Corinthians 6:19

My Heart

You Are My Redeemer, and You Live in My Heart

Your Spirit has taken up residence in my very soul. My lips will glorify Your Holy Presence within me because Your love is better than life. I am thankful to be consumed by the God of this universe. That inconceivable thought alone makes my heart sing. I rejoice that You have allowed Your Spirit to inhabit me. I am overjoyed that You chose to save me and transform my life. I can make it through each day knowing You are living in my heart. No other thing can even compare to this feeling of acceptance and love that I have in You, my Creator. My heart is filled with the satisfaction of knowing You are here with me.

Thank You for completing my heart . . .

Read:
Proverbs 3:5, Romans 8:28, James 4:8

Faithfulness

You Are What Faithful Looks Like, My Friend and Savior

I call to You, Lord. You answer me. You come to me and meet me where I am. I rest in the assurance that each time I open my mouth to call out to You, whether in trouble, need, or in praise and thanksgiving, You answer my cry and abundantly pour out Your Spirit on me. I am overwhelmed at Your loyalty to me. Sometimes it looks as though You are not answering me. It may even look like You are working in a way I do not understand. It is in these times that I must remember to trust You with all my heart and know that You make all things work together for my good. Your Word has given me assurance that when I come close to You, You will come close to me. Thank You, Jesus, for allowing me to have full access to You.

Even more, I thank You for answering me faithfully . . .

Read:
Psalm 85:2; Psalm 91:1–4; Isaiah 51:16

Covered

Lord, You Set the Heavens in Place and Laid the Foundations of the Earth

You are my beloved covering, dear Father. Yes, You have put Your words in my mouth, and You cover me with the shadow of Your hand. You have covered all my sins. You are my place of refuge. You are my fortress, my God, in whom I trust. You have covered me with Your feathers, and under Your wing I find refuge. I am concealed in Your everlasting love. You extend Your mercy and grace to me in all my shortcomings. You spread Your forgiveness over my entire being. You protect me from danger and shelter me from the storm. Thank You for being my safe haven. Thank You for being a protective sanctuary.

Thank You for being my blessed covering . . .

Read:
Psalm 24:1–6

Establishment

How Wonderful is the Work of Your Hands, Great and Mighty God

The earth is Yours, and everything in it. Myself and all who live here belong to You, Father. You founded the world upon the seas and established it upon the waters. I stand in Your holy place with clean hands and a pure heart because of Your faithful forgiveness. I receive blessing from You, Lord, and vindication from You, my God and my Savior. This generation seeks Your face. May we rest in Your peace together and pour out Your love richly on those surrounding us. Thank You for standing on the heights with us.

Thank You for the awesome place You have established for us . . .

Read:
Isaiah 64:8; Jeremiah 18:6; 2 Corinthians 4:6–7

The Potter's Hands

You Are the Great Potter, Lord, and You Are Worthy to be Praised

I am the work of Your hand. You have the right to make and mold this lump of clay into what You have predestined me to be. I thank You that You are teaching me each day to let the light shine that You have placed in my heart. Through Jesus, You have given me the light of the knowledge of the glory of God. May Your light in me shine brighter moment by moment. May I allow it to shine into a world of darkness. Thank You for entrusting me with this destiny. Thank You for helping me to believe in myself.

Thank You for sculpting something beautiful out of the ground . . .

Read:
Psalm 119:76; John 14:16–18

Comfort

You Are My Comforter, Lord

It is such a small word with such an enormous purpose. You are the creator of comfort, and You know the exact areas of my life where I need to be comforted the most. You give me hope in my times of grief and pain. You soothe the aching in my soul. I find my comfort in Your unfailing love for me. This is a promise Your Word has given to me, and I believe it with all my heart. Thank You for giving me this desire to have dependence on You.

Thank You for being my safe place to run to where I know I can receive comfort time and time again . . .

Read:
Psalm 3 & 4

Shield

Lord, You Are a Shield for Me

You are the One who lifts my head high. Your blessings are on me because I belong to You, God. Thank You for hearing me when I call to You. Thank You for giving me relief from my distress. You have set me apart for Yourself. The light of Your face shines upon me. When I lie down and sleep, it is in peace. You make me dwell in safety. I wake in the morning because You are sustaining me. You protect me and defend me. You are guarding me no matter what may come toward me. Thank You for bestowing Your glory on me. I do not fear. You are with me. Thank You for protection.

Thank You for shielding me . . .

Read:
Zephaniah 1:7; Ephesians 1:18

Consecrated

I Have Been Created and Consecrated by You, Lord

I lift up praises to You, God, the One who created everything. I am near to Your heart. You have extended the invitation to me. You have requested me to share in Your glorious riches. You have enlightened the eyes of my heart. I know the hope to which You have called me. Thank You for setting me apart and dedicating me to Your service. I am honored. I am devoted to Your purposes. I am so thankful that I matter to You. Pleasure and reward are surely mine. Thank You for holding me in such high regard. Thank You for inviting me in, Lord.

Thank You for consecrating me to the highest places with You. . .

Read:
Psalm 25:21; Lamentations 3:21–26

Hope

I Bow to the God of My Salvation and Offer Praises

Yes, I worship the great Lord who gives me hope. It is because of Your great love for me, Father, that I am not consumed in the pit of self-pity. You have great compassion on me, and You never fail me. You are my portion, therefore, I will wait for You. You are good to me because I have placed my hope in You. It is good for me to wait quietly and seek You. I will empty myself of the things of this world. I will repent, and You will forgive. You will fill me as I sit peacefully and trust in You. My hope is in You, Father. In You is where I place my trust. Thank You for my Salvation. Thank You for promises.

Thank You for giving me an eager heart that awaits a plethora of heavenly blessings . . .

Read:
John 8:34–47; Acts 7:34

Accepted and Free

You Have Accepted Me, Lord

You can see me. You hear me, and You come to give me freedom. I am not a slave to sin. I belong to the One who sets me free. I know that You came from God, Jesus. I know that He sent You to me. I hear what You say, and I love Your words. Everything You say is true, and I will not listen to the lies of the enemy. No accuracy is in satan, the father of lies. He does not hold to the truth. I believe in You, Jesus. I believe that I belong to God. I have a permanent place in Your family, and I will be with You forever.

Jesus, You have set me free from all things of this world, and I am free indeed . . .

Read:
Exodus 24:15–18; Hebrews 12:26–29

Consuming Fire

You Are a Consuming Fire, God Almighty

I worship You with reverence and awe. Your Kingdom cannot be shaken! For what cannot be shaken will always remain. Praise You, Lord! You have created me to be consumed by Your presence. My desire is to go up on the mountain and enter into communion with You. You will sustain me. May Your glory settle on me as we share in our mountaintop experiences together. It is in this place that I can hear most clearly from You, Jesus. Thank You for being my consuming fire.

Thank You for Your continual presence
burning in my heart and soul . . .

Read:
2 Corinthians 4:18; Ephesians 2:10

Focus

My Eyes Are Focused on You Today, Father

You created my eyes to see Your beauty. You strategically place people and things in my path that bring eternal blessing to me if I but recognize what You lay before me. I will search for hidden treasures throughout my day. Other people will also greatly benefit from Your riches when I am alert and I can discern what You have prepared for me. You give me the tools I need to accomplish Your works as I sit in Your presence attentive to Your desires for me. Thank You for filling me with Your Holy Spirit. Thank You for helping me remain in what is eternal. Thank You for keeping my eyes focused on the most important influence. Lord, You are the one thing that matters the most to me.

Thank You for directing me toward the center of who You are . . .

Read:
Psalm 92

Life

I Exalt You Forever, O Lord

It is so good to praise You, Father! It brings life, healing and blessing to my world. I will praise You for the rest of my life. You have made me flourish like a palm tree. I will still bear fruit in old age. I will stay fresh and green proclaiming that You are my Rock. I will proclaim Your love in the morning and Your faithfulness at night. The works of Your hands are great, and Your thoughts are profound. You, Lord, make me glad by Your deeds. I want to praise You because You are so beautiful in all Your ways. Thank You for being praiseworthy. You make it so easy for me to worship You, Father. Thank You for bringing life to me. I am fresh and new each day because of You, Jesus.

Thank You for caring for me and for nurturing me . . .

Read:
Deuteronomy 32:4; Job 36:4; Psalm 19:7; Isaiah 25:1

Perfection

Your Plans Are Perfect, Lord

Your way is perfect. You have perfect knowledge. Your laws are perfect. You are perfect in beauty, and You shine forth in perfection. I will exalt You and praise Your name. In perfect faithfulness You have done wonderful things. You are calling me to this perfection. I am to love my enemies and pray for those who persecute me. I am Your child, and You are my heavenly Father. Your sun rises on the good and the evil. You send rain on the righteous and the unrighteous. I am doing no good if I only love those who love me. There is no reward in only greeting those who are my own people. Let me love those in need, Lord. I will let You be the judge. May I be perfect, as You are perfect, my God and Savior. This is what I am to strive for. This is what Your will is for me.

Thank You for calling me to a greater, more abundant life in this short amount of time I have here on Your earth . . .

Read:
2 Thessalonians 1

Worthy

May Your Name Be Glorified in Me, Lord Jesus Christ

May I be glorified in You according to Your grace. You have said that I am worthy. You are increasing my faith, dear Father. You are increasing my love for You and for others. You have placed perseverance deep within me so that I am able to endure trials and persecutions. Because I am steadfast in my ways, You will count me worthy of the Kingdom of God. You give me relief when I am troubled, and I marvel at Your glory. I believe in You, and You have made me worthy of Your calling. You will make my desire for goodness happen by Your power, through my faith, because Your judgment is right and just. Thank You for establishing this growth and desire in me.

Praise You Lord, that You say I am worthy for the Kingdom of God . . .

Read:
Proverbs 15:15; 1 Thessalonians 5:16–18;
2 Thessalonians 3:5; Hebrews 13:15

Continue

I Continually Offer a Sacrifice of Praise to You, Lord

My lips openly profess Your name. This brings joy to my soul. My cheerful heart enjoys a continual feast. I will continue to praise You, and I will continue to pray to You. I will continue in the things I know to be true. I will continue to learn from Your Word. This kind of perseverance can only come from You, Jesus. You have directed my heart into Your love and perseverance. I may get tired and weary, but You will help me to continue my praises and thanksgiving to You. You are a continuous source of strength for my tired mind and body. Thank You for this quickening of Your Spirit in me.

Thank You, Lord, for giving me the will to keep going . . .

Read:
Matthew 6:25–34

Provision

Lord, You Are Attentive to the Details of My Life

I know You are taking care of me each day. You provide for all my needs. I am not worried about what I will eat or drink. I am not worried about what I will wear. My life with You is more important than food or clothes. I am much more valuable to You than anything this world holds. I know that worrying will not add a single hour to my life. You feed the birds of the air and clothe the grass of the field. Much more are the things You have given to me. I will seek Your Kingdom first and Your righteousness. I choose not to worry, for I know You are faithful to supply all my heart desires.

Thank You, Jehovah, for gratifying my human needs . . .

Read:
Colossians 1:15–23

Established

You Have Established All Things, Including Me

You, Christ, are before all things, and in You all things hold together. You are the firstborn over all creation. By You all things were created: things in heaven and on earth, visible and invisible, whether thrones of powers or rulers or authorities; all things were created by You and for You. God is pleased to have all His fullness dwell in You and through You to reconcile to Himself all things, whether things on earth or things in heaven, by making peace through Your blood poured out on the cross. I was once alienated from You, but now You have reconciled me by Your physical body through death to present me holy in Your sight. I am without blemish! I am free from accusation! I will continue in my faith, established and firm, not moved from the hope held out in the gospel.

Thank You, Jesus . . .

Read:
Ephesians 2:13–22

Unity

I Am One With You, Christ

I praise You for Your precious blood poured out for me. I was once far away, but You brought me near, by Your blood. You are my peace, dear Lord. It is Your will that I live peacefully. I have access to the Father through You, Jesus. I am no longer a foreigner or a stranger. I am a fellow citizen with Your people, and I am a member of Your household that was built on the foundation of the apostles and prophets, with You, Jesus, as the chief cornerstone. In You this whole building is joined together and rises to become a holy temple. Thank You for building Your people together to become a dwelling in which Your Spirit is living. Thank You for unifying us, Lord.

Thank You for making us as one . . .

Read:
John 14:27; Romans 3:23;
1 Corinthians 4:21; 1 Corinthians 10:13

Thankfulness

God, You Have Given Me the Blessings of Love and Peace

When I say thank You for the things You have provided in my life, I am not always speaking of material possessions. Your blessings come in many forms and in numerous areas. I say thank You for answered prayers. I say thank You for love, and thank You for joy. I am thanking You for listening when I speak. I thank You for the presence of the Holy Spirit. Thank You for the gift of Jesus Christ and for the forgiveness of all my sin. I am grateful for Your living Word and the way Your Spirit gently corrects me when I have fallen short. The idea that You provide a way out of temptation for everyone every time is inconceivable to my mind. I am so thankful I have been selected by You, Father. Thank You for all of Your many promises I find in reading Your Word.

Thank You for salvation and for loving me . . .

Read:
Colossians 3:1–14

Chosen

I Have Been Raised With You, Christ

I have set my mind on things above, not on earthly things. I have died to self, and my life is now hidden with You, Christ, in God. I have put to death the things that belong to earthly nature. I do not walk in my old ways anymore. I have put on the new self, which is being renewed in knowledge in the image of You, my Creator. You chose me Yourself, God. I am holy and dearly loved by You. I will clothe myself with compassion, kindness, humility, gentleness and patience. I will be forgiving toward others as You have forgiven me. Over all these virtues, I will put on love, which binds them all together in perfect unity.

Thank You for choosing me to love, Jesus . . .

Read:
Proverbs 19:23;
1 Timothy 6:6; Hebrews 13:5

Contentment

You Are My Source of Contentment, Lord Jesus

Nothing in this world can satisfy the way You do. I can chase after dreams and money only to find myself wanting more, or I can rest in Your love and drink from fountains of never-ending living water and be content. I choose You, Father of heaven and earth. I have great gain being content with You. I will fear You, Lord; this leads to life. I will rest content in Your arms and be satisfied. Thank You for accepting me, Father.

You are pleased with me, and I am indulged in You . . .

Read:
1 Chronicles 28:9;
Colossians 4:2; Titus 3:8

Devotion

I Devote My Praises and Prayers to You, Yahweh

My heart is devoted to Your will. I am trusting in You, and I am devoted to doing what is good. I am devoted to choosing only to do things which are excellent and profitable for everyone. I am devoted to prayer. Through prayer all things come into order. I am devoted to being watchful and thankful. I am ready to serve You with wholehearted devotion. I am devoted to having a sound and willing mind. You understand my every motive behind all of my thoughts. I have sought You, and You have set Your purity in my soul.

Thank You for devoting me unto Yourself, dear heavenly Father, as I devote myself to You . . .

Read:
Isaiah 64:8;
1 Thessalonians 5:18; 2 Peter 1:3

Thanksgiving

I Give Thanks to You Today, Father

You are the source of everything that inhabits my life. You are the giver of life. My days are filled with blessings from You, Father, and I praise You for it! I am the work of Your hand. Thank You for showing me how to give thanks in all circumstances. Even when things are not going my way, You have this delicate way of reminding me to be thankful for the little and big things. Thank You for being so understanding and patient with me. I am a work in progress, and I am so thankful my life is in the hands of the One who can mold me into the shape You want me to be. Your divine power has given me everything I need for a godly life through the knowledge You have given me. You have called me by Your own glory and goodness. I am thankful to You, Mighty God.

Thank You for loving me, Lord . . .

Read:
Jonah 2:6–9

Salvation

You Are My Savior, Yahweh

I praise the One who delivered me from confinement! Thank You for opening the eyes of my heart and pouring salvation into my soul. When my life was ebbing away, I remembered You, Lord. My prayer rose to You, and You brought my life up from the pit, O Lord my God. This world is temporary, ever-changing, empty and fugacious. I am merely passing through. I realize I am an alien here with a purpose to fulfill in Christ Jesus. I will not cling to worthless idols, but I will sing a song of praise to The One who has brought Salvation to me. I will never forfeit the grace You offer. Yes, a song of thanksgiving will ever be on my lips. Thank You for rescuing Your child from peril and bringing me to safety.

Thank You for being my personal Savior . . .

Read:
Psalm 46:10

Your Voice

Master, You Are the One Who Speaks to My Heart Continually

I long to hear Your voice, Father. It is my desire to walk with You in the cool of the day. I am being still, and I know that You are God. I am clearing all thoughts in my mind. I want there to be room for You to speak and for me to listen. I take a few deep breaths, and all thoughts are gone. Only You fill the chamber of my mind. In this quiet and restful moment, I am able to connect with You like never before. This is where I want to be. I am attentive to Your influence. You have many wonderful and satisfying thoughts for me.

Thank You, God, for allowing me to hear Your voice . . .

Read:
1 Samuel 3

Listening

Lord, Thank You for Revealing Your Word to Me

Thank You for calling out to me as You called to Your prophet Samuel. I am most grateful that I was able to hear You calling me amidst all the distractions of this world. I say to You now, "Here I am. Speak, Lord, for Your servant is listening." You are with me as I grow, just as You were with Samuel as he grew. You have many special words for me to speak to others. I will choose to impart Your divine wisdom on others as You call me to do so. I will not keep Your goodness to myself. You have called me to share with the world what I have received from You. Thank You for revealing Yourself to me through Your Word.

Thank You for choosing me to listen to Your instruction . . .

Read:
1 Chronicles 29:11;
Psalm 147:5; Proverbs 24:5

Power and Authority

God, You Are Omnipotent, Omnipresent, and Omniscient

You are almighty and infinite in power. You have great and unlimited authority over all. I humbly acknowledge Your greatness. I am pleased to have You as Lord of my life. I am grateful to be under Your leadership. You are everywhere at the same time, always. Your presence is endless. Far and wide, You are in all places. Lord, You know all things. You have complete and unlimited understanding. You created understanding and wisdom. Your knowledge is immeasurable and vast. I also have great power and wisdom through Jesus Christ. My strength is increased through my knowledge of Jesus. I am thankful for Your awareness of all things in my life. Thank You for being everywhere, all the time.

Thank You for managing all things with Your infinite power and authority . . .

Read:
Psalm 23; John 10:1–4

Shepherd

You Are My Shepherd, Lord

I know Your voice. You call me Your own. You go ahead of me, and I follow You. You call me by name and lead me out. I am not left wanting for anything. I lie down in green pastures. You lead me beside quiet waters. You restore my soul. You guide me in paths of righteousness. Even though I walk through the valley of the shadow of death, I fear no evil. You are with me. Your rod and staff comfort me. You prepare a table before me in the presence of my enemies. You anoint my head with oil. My cup overflows. Goodness and love follow me every day, and I will dwell in Your house forever.

Thank You for being my shepherd, dear Lord . . .

Read:
Matthew 14:15–21; John 4:4–30

Miracles

You Have Done Marvelous Things, Lord

I praise You for the miracles You have shown me. They are many. I remember the things You have brought me through, and my heart is filled with gratitude and love for You, my King. I will continue to praise You for the things You are going to do in my life. There are many good days ahead of me. When I am hungry, You feed me as You fed the five thousand. When I am thirsty, You give me living water as You gave the woman at the well. Nothing can satisfy like You, Jesus. Your glory is being continuously revealed through Your miracles.

Thank You for doing miraculous things . . .

Read:
Job 8:21, Psalm 90:14

Joy

Lord, You Are the One That Brings Joy to My Heart Continually

I praise Your name because without Your Holy Spirit living in me this life would be a dry desert land. Your living waters have burst into my soul and quenched this thirsty heart. I did not know of the ways that I longed to be satisfied by You until You filled my mouth with laughter and my lips with shouts of joy.

Thank You for satisfying me in the morning with Your unfailing love so that I may sing for joy and be glad all of my days . . .

Read:
Acts 17:24–28

Lord Almighty

You Are the God That Made the World and Everything in it

You are the Lord of heaven and of earth. You cannot be contained, Lord Almighty. You need nothing because You are everything. You give all mankind life and breath and everything we need to survive. You made every nation. You chose every person to inhabit Your earth and put them in the exact places in which they are. You have chosen me to be exactly where I am. I seek You, and I reach out for You. You are not far from me. I have found You, and I live and move and have my being in You, Father. I am Your offspring. I am so secure in these thoughts. This is my hope.

Thank You, Jesus, for being my Lord . . .

Read:
Psalm 30

Rejoice

I Exalt You, Lord

I sing praises to Your holy name. You make me feel secure. I will never be shaken. You have lifted me out of the depths. You made my royal mountain stand firm. Nothing is gained if I am silent, so I call to You for help and You heal me. Your favor lasts a lifetime. You cause me to stand firm. You have been merciful to me in my times of trouble, and You have turned my wailing and weeping into rejoicing and dancing. You clothe me with joy, and my heart sings to You. Thank You for setting me in security with You forever.

I will give You thanks forever . . .

Read:
John 15:11; John 16:24; Philippians 2:1–2; James 1:4

Complete

My Joy is Complete in You, Jesus

Nothing can take away my joy! I rejoice in You! You complete me! I am united with You, Christ Jesus. I am encouraged and comforted by Your love. My joy is complete by being like-minded with You. We are one in Spirit and purpose. I will persevere through my day. I will ask for things in Your name. I will be mature and complete, not lacking anything. I will receive what You have planned for me today. This day can only be complete with You as my Savior and Friend.

Thank You for making me complete . . .

Read:
Proverbs 3:26; Isaiah 32:17; Philippians 3:3;
1 John 5:14

Confidence

You Are My Confidence, Lord, Jesus

With You, I have certainty. Because I am righteous in Your eyes, I will have peace, quietness and confidence forever. I have put my trust in You, Father. My confidence is in You alone. You will keep my foot from being snared. I put no confidence in the flesh. I have the confidence I need to approach You, Jesus. Your Word tells me that if I ask anything according to Your will, You hear me. I know that You will answer, and I will have what You want me to have according to Your will. Thank You for giving me this great assurance in You, Lord.

Thank You for making Yourself available for me to exercise my hopefulness . . .

Read:
Psalm 46:10; Psalm 95:6–7; Romans 12:1

Devoted to Worship

Worshiping You is Important to Me, God

I bow down at Your feet, and I am still before You, knowing that You are my God and my Savior. I exalt You, Father of all Your creation. I am devoted to You. I offer my body as a living sacrifice to You, God. This spiritual act of worship is holy and pleasing to You. I am here to worship You. Other tasks on my daily list can wait. This priority is the most important thing I can do today. Thank You for meeting with me and allowing me to make this sacrifice to You.

Thank You for granting me the favor of worshiping You, Lord . . .

Read:
**Psalm 72:19; Luke 8:17;
1 Corinthians 10:26; Ephesians 1:19–20**

Glory

Glory To You, Lord

You have done great and mighty things! The earth is filled with Your glory! You are the master of the universe! All things come together and praise Your holy Name. Nothing happens in all creation without Your divine approval. You have established authority and power on the earth through Your children. Your Spirit living within me gives me the same power that raised Jesus from the dead! I can do all things through my heavenly Father, who chose me to be a shining light in this world of darkness. You are on Your throne, God. You reign forever. Thank You for injecting Your power and authority into these dry bones. Thank You for bringing me to life through Jesus!

Glory belongs to You, Father. Hallelujah . . .

Read:
1 Chronicles 16:24–27; Psalm 19:1; Psalm 71:8

Declarations

I Declare Your Glory, Lord of All the Earth

I declare praises to You, Father! You are most worthy of all of my praise. I will announce Your splendor all day long. I will make declarations of thanksgiving no matter the circumstances. You are Lord of everything. My mouth is filled with Your praise. You have permitted me the advantage of making bold and confident declarations of praise to You because You are so holy and righteous. You are my mighty King of all Kings. The heavens declare Your glory, God. The skies proclaim the work of Your hands. You have made Yourself so evident to the nations.

Thank You for giving me authority to declare praises to You, my Father . . .

Read:
John 1:1–18

Light

Jesus, You Are the True Light That Has Come Into the World

I praise You for granting me the position of being Your child. I am born of You, God. You give Your light to every man. May the world recognize and receive You, Father. You are full of grace and truth. You have revealed Yourself to me. From the fullness of Your grace, I have received Your light through one blessing after another. I know my Father in heaven because I have learned who He is through the flesh of Jesus Christ, the Light of the world. Thank You for Your Word. Thank You for sending the Light to me.

Thank You, Lord, for inhabiting me with Your Light . . .

Read:
Ephesians 2:4–8

Grace

You Are Alive, Jesus

I worship and adore You, my King! And because You are alive, I am alive! Since You have so much great love and rich mercy for me, You have made me alive with You, Christ. Even when I was dead in transgressions, Your grace saved me. Thank You, Jesus. I am raised up and seated with You in heavenly realms. You will show me Your incomparable riches of Your grace in the coming ages. I have seen a certain kindness expressed only through You, Jesus. I am alive because You have saved me by grace through my faith in You. I did not come up with this idea. This has been Your plan from the beginning. Grace is given to me as a gift from You, O God.

Thank You for investing in me eternally . . .

Read:
Ephesians 1:11–14

Chosen

I Am Thankful That My Hope is in You, Jesus

You have chosen me for the praise of Your glory! According to Your plan, I was predestined by You. You work out everything in conformity with the purpose of Your will. I am included in Christ because I heard the message of truth and believed. I am marked in You with a seal which is the promise of the Holy Spirit living in me. This is a deposit that guarantees my inheritance in heaven. I am Your possession, Lord. I am secure in who I am through You, Father. Thank You for promising me the special privilege of being a part of Your Kingdom. Thank You for exposing me to Your truth.

Thank You for marking me and choosing me . . .

Read:
Luke 9:23

Disciple

I Am Your Disciple, Jesus

I know there is a cost for following You, Father. It is a huge daily sacrifice to carry out Christian activity in a day. Your footsteps can be much larger than I anticipate when I set out to do the work of a disciple. Many times I find myself fumbling through scattered words to try to somehow put together uplifting expressions that will hopefully edify those You have placed in my pathway. My dependence on You is essential as a supporter of the gospel. You have carried me through many moments of victory and defeat as well. I am eternally grateful to a God that never fails me.

Thank You for helping me as I disciple a fallen world and help You bring them the hope of salvation . . .

Read:
Psalm 145:1–7

Praise

I Belong To You, Jesus

You have captured my heart, and Your Spirit is arising from this individual structure You created. I am taken by Your beauty and grace. You have made a way for me, and I am at peace. I will bless You every day, Father, and I will praise Your name forever and ever. Each day I meditate on the glorious splendor of Your majesty. I speak of the might of Your awesome works. One generation will tell of Your works to another. One generation will praise Your name to another. I will be faithful to utter the memory of Your great goodness. I will celebrate Your abundance. Thank You for encircling me with Your peace. Thank You for claiming me.

I am looking forward to forever with You . . .

Read:
Hebrews 12:3–13

Discipline

Thank You for Disciplining Me, Lord

I praise You that You are making me into what You want me to be, rather than what I think I should be. Your discipline is necessary for me to live a victorious Christian life. I am dependent on You for discipline. It is what keeps me moving in the right direction. No discipline seems pleasant at the time. It is downright painful sometimes. However, later on it produces a harvest of righteousness and peace for those of us who have been trained by it. I know You are disciplining me for my own good, Father. I thank You for it, and I love You for it. I will strengthen my feeble arms and weak knees. I will make level paths for my feet. I will not be disabled, but healed! I know that You love and accept me because You discipline me. I accept this truth. Thank You for caring so much for me, Jesus.

Thank You for disciplining me . . .

Read:
Psalm 145:16; Luke 6:21; Romans 8:11;
1 Thessalonians 5:18

Satisfied

I Am Satisfied With You, Heavenly Father

I eat what You provide, and I am satisfied. You are the right amount of everything I need! I Praise You, Jesus! I need nothing more than Your Spirit living inside of me to have a heart of gratitude. You open Your hand and satisfy the desires of every living thing. I am thankful for the intimate moments we share together. I am overjoyed at having a fresh encounter with You daily. This kind of love is what keeps me going and gets me through this life of challenges. It is pleasing for me to walk with You, and talk with You, throughout my day. This keeps us in close relationship. I am thankful we can communicate regularly.

Thank You for satisfying my every desire . . .

Read:
Psalm 125:1–2; Psalm 126:1–3;
Habakkuk 3:18; Haggai 1:7

Joy

I Rejoice in You Today, Lord

I am joyful in You, God my Savior. You have done great things for me, and I am filled with joy and laughter. I will give careful thought to my ways. I will trust that the path You have for me today is put in place by Your mighty hand. When I trust in You, Lord, I am like a mountain that cannot be shaken but endures forever. I am strong in You, Jesus. You surround me now and forevermore. My arms and my mind are strengthened and steadfast because of You. I will not be moved. Thank You for giving me joy in the morning. Thank You for giving me the ability to endure my day.

Thank You for the happiness and joy I clinch tightly to and have to look forward to each day just from knowing You . . .

Read:
Psalm 130:7; Psalm 132:14–15, 18

Redeemed

O Lord, You Are Everything That Satisfies Me

I give honor and praises to my Sovereign God. You have fully redeemed me. You have given me complete forgiveness of all my transgressions. You have desired that I be Your dwelling place. You have chosen me, and You sit enthroned in my heart. You desire me, and You bless me with abundant provisions. You have placed a resplendent crown upon my head. I am beaming with supernatural radiance. Thank You for claiming what was lost and giving me new life. Thank You for satisfying Your child.

Thank You for making me new . . .

Read:
1 Kings 8:23; Psalm 27:11; Matthew 7:14

Covenant of Love

I Open My Eyes to Your Beauty, and You Fill My Mouth With a Thousand Praises

O Lord, there is no God like You in heaven above or on the earth below. You keep Your covenant of love with Your servants who continue wholeheartedly in Your way. Although I am amongst much conflict in my daily activities and thoughts, You are helping me to act in harmony together with the saints You have chosen. You give us the ability to uphold the precepts of the gospel. You have placed love in our hearts so that the world may see You through Your people. Thank You for helping me to continue to walk the straight and narrow path that leads to everlasting life with You.

Thank You for Your covenant of love . . .

Read:
Ephesians 4:25; Colossians 3:15–17

Member

I Am a Member of Your Body, Lord

I will let Your peace rule in my heart. You have called me to peace as a member of one body with the saints. I am thankful in all I do because of the love You have shown the world. Your Word is richly dwelling in me because You have given me Your wisdom that teaches and admonishes. I will teach and admonish others, in Your name. I will put off falsehood and speak truthfully to my neighbor. May I have gratitude in my heart in whatever I do. I choose to share Your love with the world around me because we are all members of this world together. My membership in the body of Christ, however, sets me apart from worldly ways. I take this position with honor because You have placed me here. Thank You for giving me a place in Your Kingdom. May You touch many lives through me.

Thank You for making me a member of Your eternal family . . .

Read:
Psalm 94:11; Proverbs 14:15; Isaiah 55:8–9; Philippians 4:8

Thoughts

Hallelujah to You, Lord

You give me pure thoughts. I love to think on things that are true, noble, right, pure, lovely, admirable, excellent and praiseworthy. It is only because of You, Jesus, that I am able to do this. You have caused me to be prudent so that I may give thought to my steps. I am thankful that You know my thoughts, Lord. It keeps me accountable, and our thoughts are vastly different. Your thoughts and ways are much higher than mine. I thank You for Your living Word that is sharper than any double-edged sword. I am thankful it judges the thoughts and attitudes of my heart. There is nothing in me that You do not know about, and I am thankful for the accountability relationship I have with You.

Thank You for knowing my deepest, most secret thoughts . . .

Read:
John 12:38, 44–50

Message

Lord, Your Message is Powerful

It is through Jesus Christ that I have heard the message of Salvation. I believe in You, Jesus. I believe in the One who sent You. You have come into the world as a light. Your arm has been revealed to me. I do not continue to live in darkness because I believe in the Light of the world. You did not come to judge the world, but to save it. Your commands lead to eternal life. Thank You for choosing to share the message with me. Thank You for the revealing of God through the message. I love the message.

Thank You for allowing me to continue sharing the message . . .

Read:
Luke 1:34–35, 77–79

Salvation

You Are the Savior, Jesus

You created salvation for me and for all the people of Your earth. You gave me knowledge of Salvation through the forgiveness of my sins. I was living in darkness and because of Your tender mercy the rising sun shined down on me. You guide my feet into the path of peace. You saw that I was in need of a Savior. You sent Jesus, Your one and only Son, to be born of a virgin to save me from my sins. You teach me how to live out my Salvation each day as I read about the miraculous things recorded in Your Word. Thank You for bringing Salvation to this world. Thank You for saving me from my sins. Thank You for giving me eternal life with You.

Thank You for being my Savior . . .

Read:
Luke 1:46–53

Mary's Song

My Soul Glorifies You, Lord

My spirit rejoices in God my Savior. You are mindful of me, Lord. I am blessed. You are the Mighty One, and You have done great things for me. Your name is Holy. You extend Your mercy to those who fear You, from generation to generation. You perform mighty deeds with Your arm. You scatter the proud and bring down rulers from their thrones, yet You lift up the humble. You fill the hungry with good things. I bless Your Holy name. Thank You, Lord, for being merciful to me. Thank You for teaching me about humility. Thank You for Your Word that gives me hope and a song in my heart.

Thank You for Mary's song . . .

Read:
Matthew 1:23; Luke 2:14, 52

Jesus

Glory to God in the Highest, and on Earth Peace to Men on Whom His Favor Rests

You are Immanuel. God, You are with us! Praise and glory belong to You, God, for sending Your Son Jesus to be the Savior of the world. Thank You for giving us a picture of who You truly are through Jesus, our Lord and Savior. Thank You for that blessed night in Bethlehem. Thank You for the precious baby who grew in wisdom and stature and gained favor with God and men. He taught the world how to live and how to love. We are blessed to live in Your world, and we give You honor and glory for Your graciousness to us for such a valuable gift. Your love and tenderness toward Your people is revealed through the birth and life of Jesus.

Thank You for Jesus . . .

Read:
Psalm 103:1; Isaiah 42:10–13; John 14:6

Praise

How Amazing You Are, God

How radiant and glorious! Your splendor covers the earth You created! I proclaim Your praise in all the land. I sing for joy and shout from the mountaintops! How majestic and holy You are, my warrior and champion! May I never be silent, but stir up Your zeal within me so that I may always raise my voice in a new song for the glory of You, Lord. I will praise You to the ends of the earth. I will never hold myself back from honoring and praising You, God. You are the Savior of the world. You are the way, the truth, and the life. There is nothing better. There is nothing greater. Everything I am is because You created every part of me. All praise, honor, glory and love belong to You, precious Father.

Thank You for being so amazingly praiseworthy . . .

Read:
James 1:2–3; 1 Peter 4:12–19

Christian

I Rejoice in You, Christ

I willingly participate in the sufferings of being a Christian. I try not to be surprised at the painful trials I endure for Your names sake. It is not a new or strange thing to suffer for You, Lord. Your Word clearly tells me this is part of eternal life. If I am insulted because of You, I am blessed, for the Spirit of glory and of God rests on me. I praise You that I am a Christian and that I bear Your name. However, I will be overjoyed when Your glory is fully revealed. I commit myself to my faithful Creator, and I will continue to do good. When sufferings and troubles of any kind come my way, I will pray and consider it an opportunity for great joy. When my faith is tested, my endurance has a chance to grow.

Thank You, Lord, for chances to cultivate my Christianity . . .

Read:
Romans 3:24 & 6:14; 2 Corinthians 8:9;
Ephesians 1:7–8; 2 Thessalonians 2:16–17

Amazing Grace

Praise You, Lord, for Amazing Grace

I am justified freely by Your grace through the redemption that came by Jesus Christ. I am far from perfect, and I mess up quite frequently. I even feel guilt and shame for my shortcomings. However, I have been given a free gift through You, Jesus. Sin will not be my master! Hallelujah! I am not under the law. I am under grace. Thank You, Jesus! Though You were rich, You became poor. You did this for my sake, so that through Your poverty I might become rich. I am redeemed through Your blood, and my sins are forgiven. You have lavished Your riches on me with all wisdom and understanding. My heart is encouraged by Your love and grace. Thank You for strengthening me in every good deed and word.

This is amazing grace . . .

Read:
1 Chronicles 16:34; Psalm 9:7;
Psalm 33:11; Psalm 86:12; Hebrews 13:8

Forever

You are forever, Lord!

Your love endures forever. You reign forever. Your plans will stand firm forever. You are the same yesterday and today and forever. I will glorify Your name forever. I really cannot even fathom what forever looks like because I am so small and so dependent on You, Father. I *do* know that You hold forever in Your hands, and I am trusting my forever to You. In a world of such uncertainty, You are the One thing that gives me hope that I will be with You forever. You are what I put my trust in to hold me in Your arms forever. Thank You for being in charge of my forever. Thank You for enduring and reigning forever.

Thank You for this hope I have because I have trusted that I will be with You forever . . .

Read:
Deuteronomy 6:3–7; Psalm 77:14, 78:1–4

Our God

You Are the God Who Performs Miracles

Your power is on display for all to see. Your commands are great, and You are wise. You have given us much strength to live by, and You have provided wisdom for our hearts to receive. Your ways are holy, God. We read and listen to Your teaching. You open Your mouth and utter hidden things from of old. We will tell the next generation the praiseworthy deeds of You, Lord. We will be careful to obey Your commands so that it may go well with us and that we may greatly increase in the land. We will love You with all our heart, soul, and strength. We have Your ways impressed upon our hearts, and we will talk about them when we sit at home and when we walk along the road, when we lie down and when we rise. All You are is demonstrated to us through the love of Jesus Christ.

Thank You, Father, for making Yourself visible to us through Your son . . .

Read:
Matthew 28:20; Revelation 1:5–8, 17–18;
Revelation 22:20–21

Come, Lord Jesus!

You Are Lord, Jesus Christ

You are the faithful Witness and the Ruler of the kings of the earth. You have freed me from my sin by Your blood. You have made me to be a kingdom and priest to serve Your God and Father. To You be glory and power for ever and ever! Amen. You will come on the clouds, and every eye will see You. Even those that pierced You. You are the Alpha and the Omega. You are the First and the Last. You are the Living One! My hope is in You, Lord. Praise be to You God, my Father. You are the One to come! Amen! Come, Lord Jesus, and Your grace is with all Your people.

You are with us always, to the very end of the age . . .

Printed in the United States
By Bookmasters